THE LITTLE BLACK BOOK OF THE BEAUTY BIZ VOLUME 1.

The secrets of business critical to a salon's success.

Charles Read
MBA, CPA, USTCP, USMC, IRSAC
26-year Business Owner

Devon Kirk
Salon and Spa Marketing Expert
30-year Licensed Esthetician
7-year Day Spa Owner

Introduction

Charles Read has been a leader in business for over 50-years. As a 26-year successful business owner, he knows the secrets to success. But it's his skills as a CPA and U.S. Tax Court Practitioner that led him to identify critical components in business setup and to deal with Federal and State agencies that have kept most business owners in the dark. This darkness costs small business owners dearly every single year.

Devon Kirk has been a medical esthetician for 30-years. She has been licensed as an esthetician in Pennsylvania, Delaware, Georgia, and Texas. She owned a successful day spa for seven years. Unfortunately, she was unaware of some of the information in this book, and it cost her almost $3,500 in IRS penalties. Had she known how to deal with the IRS, she would have been able to abate almost or all of the penalties and interest.

When Mrs. Kirk closed her business and moved to Texas. She decided to put her business degree and marketing expertise to use and work in an industry that helps small business. That's how Mr. Read and Mrs. Kirk met. Mrs. Kirk interviewed for Mr. Read at his business, GetPayroll, and became his Director of Marketing.

Soon after they realized their common goal, and after hearing Mrs. Kirks woes with payroll and dealing with IRS penalties (an IRS agent actually came to Mrs. Kirks business and presented her with papers). They decided to embark on educating salon and spa business owners on the secrets of business they need to know to be successful.

This book dives into issues that no one prepares you for, dealing with the IRS, States and Local tax agencies. Did you know that more than 75% of small businesses have 1 to 10 employees, and that number jumps to over 90% for small businesses with up to 20 employees? The IRS is rife with opportunity to target small businesses for errors or missed due dates and penalize them for the smallest mistake. Even if you do it all right, the IRS makes egregious errors on a daily basis, and you may be in the position to have to prove your innocence based off one of their mistakes.

What if you categorized your new hire incorrectly as an independent contractor when she is really an employee? Did you know that if you supply them with anything, then they may be considered by the IRS as an employee? Mr. Read helps clear the air on this, so you know exactly what to do and how to treat your new hire.

What do you do if you if an ex-employee files for unemployment? Mr. Read shares specific steps to avoid unemployment claims. Be aware that if you have a 1099 contractor attempt to file unemployment a case may be opened against your business. Mr. Read prepares you for this possibility too.

One of the most important documents you can have is your Employee Manual. It is your safety net against employee issues and protects you against unemployment claims. You'll want to have each staff member sign an acknowledgment document too. A non-compete agreement can be included in the handbook. We'll give you everything you need to include plus a template to customize to your business.

We've included interview do's and don'ts, questions you can't legally ask anymore and legal alternatives plus an annual calendar with all things payroll so you'll never miss a deadline. Lastly, Mrs. Kirk shares her expertise in marketing: How to successfully create your brand and start building your social media presence. She has noticed so many salons missing out on creating their specific brand that speaks volumes about their businesses. She knew she was on the right track when two salons in the area chose to completely copy her brand colors, voice style, layout, and imagery - yes this stuff actually happens in business.

Use this book as a reference tool for your business. Highlight and bookmark pages that you'll return to time and again. You'll be glad you did.

Table of Contents

How to Pay an Independent Contractor or an Employee and Everything In-between

I t's confusing, right? Do you classify your new hire as a W2 employee and pay taxes on them or do you classify them as a 1099 and "save money" on your payroll taxes. Notice I put quotes on saving money. If you misclassify and get caught, you'll pay more in penalties than you did in "saving money."

In order to know how to pay workers for their services, you must first understand what their classification is. **One of the things you need to know is what business relationship exists between you and the worker performing services for your company**.

An employee can be classified as one of the following:

1. **An employee (also known as a common-law employee)**: Under common-law rules, anyone who performs services for you is your employee if you can control what will be done and how it will be done. This is so even when you give the employee freedom of action. What matters is that you have the right to control the details of how the services are performed.[1]

1 Part 1- Independent Contractor Vs. An Employee .., http://www.getpayroll.com/payroll-academy/pa170801 (accessed November 3, 2017).

2. **An independent contractor**: People such as doctors, dentists, veterinarians, lawyers, accountants, contractors, subcontractors, public stenographers, and auctioneers who are in an independent trade, business, or profession in which they offer their services to the general public are generally independent contractors. However, whether these people are independent contractors or employees depends on the facts of each case. [2]

The general rule is that an individual is an independent contractor if the payer has the right to control or direct only the result of the work and not what will be done and how it will be done.

The earnings of a person who is working as an independent contractor are subject to Self-Employment Tax. [3]

3. **A statutory employee**: If workers are independent contractors under the common law rules, such workers may nevertheless be treated as employees by statute (statutory employees) for certain employment tax purposes if they fall within any one of the following four categories and meet the three conditions described under Social Security and Medicare taxes, below.

   • A driver who distributes beverages (other than milk) or meat, vegetable, fruit, or bakery products; or who picks up and delivers laundry or dry cleaning, if the driver is your agent or is paid on commission.

   • A full-time life insurance sales agent whose principal business activity is selling life insurance or annuity contracts, or both, primarily for one life insurance company.

   • An individual who works at home on materials or goods that you supply and that must be returned to you or to a person you name if you also furnish specifications for the work to be done.

   • A full-time traveling or city salesperson who works on your behalf and turns in orders to you from wholesalers, retailers, contractors, or operators of hotels, restaurants, or other similar establishments. The goods sold must be merchandise for resale or supplies for use in the buyer's business operation. The work performed for you must be the salesperson's principal business activity. [4]

4. **A statutory nonemployee**: Direct sellers, licensed real estate agents and certain companion sitters are considered statutory nonemployees. Direct sellers and

---

2 The Irs 20 Point List For Classifying Employees | Primepay, https://primepay.com/blog/irs-20-point-list-classifying-employees (accessed November 3, 2017).

3 Clark, Kent, and Cathy Jensen. 2015. "What to Expect When the IRS Audits Your Community." PM. Public Management 97 (4). International City/County Management Association: 16.

4 Statutory Employees | Internal Revenue Service, https://www.irs.gov/businesses/small-businesses-self-employed/statutory-employee (accessed November 3, 2017).

licensed real estate agents are treated as self-employed for all Federal tax purposes, including income and employment taxes, if:

- Substantially all payments for their services as direct sellers or real estate agents are directly related to sales or other output, rather than to the number of hours worked, and

- Their services are performed under a written contract providing that they will not be treated as employees for Federal tax purposes.Companion sitters who are not employees of a companion sitting placement service are generally treated as self-employed for all federal tax purposes.[5]

5. **A government worker**: In most cases, individuals who serve as public officials are government employees. Therefore, the government entity is responsible for withholding and paying Federal income tax, social security and Medicare taxes. They must also issue a Form W-2, Wage, and Tax Statement, to a public official.[6]

Let's start with one of the thornier questions and one that has great potential for harm. Is a person working for you an employee or an independent contractor? A Quick History Lesson

What is an independent contractor you ask? There is no good answer!

Before the 20th century, this question was basically a tort law question concerning the liability of a master for their servant's actions. However, in the twentieth century, Congress adopted rules specifying the difference between an employee and an independent contractor. There has been a great deal of litigation concerning this issue and many updates of the statutes happening up to the current moment.There are also various additional regulations issued by the Treasury Department.

In the last few decades, the numbers of independent contractors have mushroomed. The reason, in many cases, is to force workers to pay for an opportunity to work rather than paying wages and overtime. The worker who purchases a "contract" to clean a building, a taxi driver who rents a cab for a twelve-hour shift. There is very little difference in the work done by these independent contractors and full-time employees doing the same job. **But the independent contractor label keeps them from getting the protection of the labor laws at the Federal and State level**; as well as denying them the right to organize into a labor union.

5 Statutory Nonemployees | Internal Revenue Service, https://www.irs.gov/businesses/small-businesses-self-employed/statutory-nonemplo (accessed November 3, 2017).

6 Tax Withholding For Government Workers | Internal Revenue ..., https://www.irs.gov/government-entities/federal-state-local-governments/tax-with (accessed November 3, 2017).

The advantages to an employer are large in using independent contractors:

- Reduced overhead costs,

- Reduced payroll taxes, and

- Reduced expenses of paying an accountant for such payroll.

There are no benefits for independent contractors: no health insurance, no vacation, no jury duty, no time off with pay.That means that the independent contractor works when the employer wants him to. There is full flexibility about when they work with no overtime pay for long hours and no pay for down times.In addition, you can many times get very experienced and well-trained contractors.If you were hiring employees, the employer would be responsible for getting them trained up.[7]

Why Does The IRS Dislike The Independent Contractor Classification?

From the IRS point of view, independent contractors have a much easier time if they choose, to cheat on their taxes.

The IRS, in Fiscal 2016, processed almost 3 billion Form 1099 information returns. All of the Form 1099 information returns have to be recorded and matched to the individual taxpayer's return. The IRS then has to select that return for an audit, catch the mismatch in the audit process, and assess the taxpayer for the unreported income and the taxes due.

There are multiple steps at which the process stated above can fail.With three billion Form 1099 information returns, there is no way to know how many of those returns are not reported on the tax return that is associated with the Form 1099 information return.

On the other hand, with about 128 million full and part-time workers in the US, the number of W2s filed was a fraction of the Form 1099 information returns filed. Also, each employee is required to attach information on their W2s to the return itself simplifying the matching process.

There is a second step in which W2s are matched to the employer-filed Form 941 quarterly wage and tax reporting.If the totals don't match, there is a department in the IRS that investigates those mismatches. The same mechanisms, however, do not exist for Form 1099 information returns.

From the businessman's point-of-view it is much easier to have an independent contractor and pay them for only the work that they do than it is to pay an employee.

7 Part 1- Independent Contractor Vs. An Employee .., http://www.getpayroll.com/payroll-academy/pa170801 (accessed November 3, 2017).

There are no taxes to deposit or forms to file quarterly, no changing deposit cycles, no State Unemployment tax to pay, no unemployment claims to fight, no benefits to pay. The employer just has to simply file 1099 for each contractor at the end of the year and one 1096 to summarize all of the contracted labor for that year.

For the Independent Contractor, all of the expenses associated with the work they do can be deducted, in full, starting with the first dollar and without any kind of limitation. I use to teach a course for crafters on "How To Live in a Deductible World." There are ways to make a lot of expenses deductible if you are an Independent Contractor. If the contractor is getting paid enough, then it even justifies paying both sides of the FICA Tax as well as self-employment tax on the Contractor's Form 1040 Federal Income Tax Return.

What Makes One Person An Independent Contractor And Another An Employee?

As much as you may think that it should be a matter of choice it really is not. There are Common and Statute rules governing the status of any particular worker. *The government simply won't let you just choose.*

Through time, the judiciary authority has identified various factors in which they felt were relevant in determining a worker's employment status.

In 1987 the IRS created a list of 20 factors they consider relevant in determining a worker's employment status after examining the case law.

The twenty items listed in the IRS Revenue Ruling 87- 41 include the following:

1. Instructions: If the employer has the right to require the worker to comply with the employer's instructions.

2. Training: If the worker can be required to attend training as to how the work is done.

3. Integration: The services performed by the work integrated into the normal operations of the business.

4. Personal Service: Does the employer require that the worker performs the services or can the worker at their own behest substitute another person?

5. Hiring, Supervising, and Paying: If the employer hires, pays, and supervises assistants for the worker rather than the worker hiring, paying and supervising his or her own assistants. This is an indication of control.

6. Continuing Relationship: That the employer and the worker maintain an ongoing and continuous relationship.

7. Set Hours of Work: The worker has established regular hours for work set by the employer.

8. Full-time Required: The worker should work full time for the employer rather than be free to work for whoever s/he wants to and whenever s/he wants to.

9. Work on Employer's Premises: The services performed by the worker are performed in facilities controlled by the employer.

10. Sequence Test: The worker performs tasks in the order that the employer specifics.

11. Reporting: The worker must submit reports either verbally or in writing on a regular basis.

12. Payment: The work is paid by a time unit (Hour/day/week/etc.) as opposed to being paid by the job.

13. Expenses: If the employer pays the expenses for the worker it leans toward an employment status.[8]

14. Tools: Normally if the worker's tools are provided this would indicate that the worker is an employee.

15. Investment: If the worker has made a significant investment in the facilities where the work is performed it indicates that the worker may be an independent contractor.

16. Profit or Loss: A worker who is an employee does not normally make a profit or a loss in addition to his normal pay.

17. One Employer: Normally a worker who performs the same service for multiple employers at the same time is indicative of an independent contractor.

18. Generally Available: If the worker makes his services available to the general public it is indicative of an independent contractor.

19. Discharge: The ability of an employer to fire a worker leans toward the worker being an employee.

20. Termination: A worker who can quit at any time indicates that the worker is an employee.

In general, answers to questions "1-16" and answers to questions "17-20" indicate an independent contractor. However, a simple majority of answers to questions "1-16 and answers to questions "17- 20" does not guarantee independent contractor treatment. Some questions are either irrelevant or of less importance because the answers may apply equally to employees and independent contractors.[9]

---

8 Part 1- Independent Contractor Vs. An Employee .., http://www.getpayroll.com/payroll-academy/pa170801 (accessed November 25, 2017).

9 Irs 20 Questions W2 Vs 1099 - Home | Gala Choruses, http://galachoruses.org/sites/default/files/IRS-20-questions-W2-vs-1099.pdf (accessed November 4, 2017).

Since 1987, the IRS has been refining and trying to implement a system that is easier to make determination than the twenty common law rules.

More recently, the IRS has identified three types of conditions that could be used in determining the status of a worker as an independent contractor or an employee, those are:

1. Behavioral control,

2. Financial control, and

3. Relationship of the parties.

The IRS makes the point that in addition to the twenty common law questions there are other factors that may be relevant to the employment status and that the weight allocated to each factor may vary based on the situation.Also, specific factors may change in relevance and weight over time and that you have to look at all the facts of every case.

In general, the following is true: Individuals who offer the services they perform in the course of their profession to the general public are normally independent contractors. Courts realize that in this day and age, highly skilled or highly educated workers don't require the minute by minute supervision of a bygone era. *So, day to day control over a worker is not necessarily helpful in determining status.*

The courts are tending to focus on the worker's ability to realize the profit or loss from their services particularly as shown by who pays expenses and who finances the business. In the end, it all falls to a single opinion of a judge. If the IRS says that your independent contractors are employees, you will have to spend time and money going to court to get that opinion overturned.

There are currently some safe harbors if you think you will have this particular problem. Talk with a CPA who understands employment tax practice they can explain what programs are in place. They change from time-to-time without warning and may have required a certain pattern of behavior to be effective.

Beware Of State Laws About Misclassification

In California, as of 1/1/12 if you misclassify a worker as an independent contractor instead of an employee, the potential fine is five to fifteen thousand dollars.Oklahoma, on the other hand, does not contain any fines for misclassification.

If you want to get a better grasp from the IRS on how they are going to classify an employee you can submit a Form SS-8 to obtain a determination from the IRS. This will take six months or more to get your answer. In the meantime, if you have chosen the wrong filing of the SS-8, the IRS is not going to relieve you of any liability. In fact, it raises a red flag to the IRS to come out and audit you.

Beware Of Ex-Independent Contractors Claiming Employee Status

If a worker files a complaint about being treated as an independent contractor instead of an employee, the IRS will ask you to fill out an IRS Form SS-8.

At that point if all your paperwork is not in the perfect order you may lose, not only the status determination but your safe harbor. If you're not sure exactly how to maintain your safe harbor for independent contract employees contact your local CPA and get on the straight and narrow.

Employment Tax Obligations: Independent Contractors

Once a determination is made (whether by the business or by the IRS), the next step is filling the appropriate forms and paying the associated taxes.

There are no tax withholdings normally for an independent contractor and no associated deposits or filing other than having to fill an annual IRS Form 1099 misc to report the payment to an independent contractor. You only need to file this return if the amount paid in the calendar year exceeds $600.00 for a particular contractor.

All the Form 1099s that were issued by the business need to be summarized in an IRS Form 1096 which accompanies the 1099s.

Employment Tax Obligations: Employees

For Employees, the procedure is much more complex and there are many additional factors that you have to consider.

Payroll Taxes: Regardless of your business form, if you are going to have employees then you will have to contend with payroll taxes. The brief summary that follows will give you some guidance in the rules and regulations of the various taxing authorities.

Available Publications: Circular E, Publication 15, Employer's Tax Guide, covers payroll tax reporting and deposit requirements and can be obtained through the local office of the Internal Revenue Service or by clicking on the link above or at the end of this chapter.[10]

---

10 Taos Business Kit, Payroll Taxes - Taoscpa.com, http://www.taoscpa.com/payroll_taxes.html (accessed November 23, 2017).

Tax Deposit Requirements: Federal income tax withheld and FICA taxes (employer and employee portion) must be deposited on a schedule according to how large your tax deposits were for the previous look back period of July 1-June 30.

When To Deposit - Taken Directly From IRS.Gov Website

You must make deposits according to one of two deposit schedules, monthly or semiweekly. The schedule you use for the current calendar year depends on the amount of taxes you reported during your lookback period. If you've filed only Form 941, the lookback period is 12 months, covering four quarters ending on June 30th of the prior year. If you filed Form 944 in either of the two previous years or you're filing Form 944 in the current year, the lookback period is the second prior calendar year. (Refer to Chapter 11 of Publication 15, [Circular E], Employer's Tax Guide.)[11]

Monthly Schedule Depositor: If you reported taxes of **$50,000 or less** during the lookback period, you're a monthly schedule depositor, and you generally must deposit your employment taxes on payments made during a given month on or before the 15th day of the following month. For example, you must deposit taxes on payments made in January by February 15. If the 15th of any calendar month falls on a Saturday, Sunday, or legal holiday, the deposit is due by the next business day.[12]

Semiweekly Schedule Depositor: If you reported taxes of **more than $50,000** for the lookback period, you're a semiweekly schedule depositor, and you generally must deposit your employment taxes based on the following schedule:

1. If your payday is on Wednesday, Thursday, and/or Friday, you must deposit these taxes by the following Wednesday.

2. If your payday is on Saturday, Sunday, Monday, and/or Tuesday, you must deposit these taxes by the following Friday.

If you're required to make a deposit on a day that's not a business day, the deposit is considered timely if you make it by the close of the next business day. A business day is any day other than a Saturday, Sunday, or legal holiday. For example, if you're required to make a deposit on a Friday and Friday is a legal holiday, the deposit will be considered timely if you make it by the following Monday (if that Monday is a business day). The term legal holiday means any legal holiday in the District of Columbia (refer to Chapter 11 of Publication 15). A statewide legal holiday, other than those listed, doesn't delay the due date of federal tax deposits. Semiweekly schedule

11 Forms 941 And 944 – Deposit Requirements, https://taxmap.irs.gov/taxmap/taxtp/Tt750_16-007.htm (accessed November 23, 2017).

12 Forms 941 And 944 – Deposit Requirements, https://taxmap.irs.gov/taxmap/taxtp/Tt750_16-007.htm (accessed November 23, 2017).

depositors have at least 3 business days to make a deposit. If any of the 3 weekdays after the end of a semiweekly period is a legal holiday, you'll have an additional day for each day that's a legal holiday to make the required deposit.[13]

One Day Depositor: If a monthly or semi-weekly depositor accumulates employment taxes of $100,000 or more during a deposit period (monthly or semi-weekly), taxes must be deposited by the next banking day.

This rule overrides the normal rules for determining the deposit dates discussed above. A monthly depositor who must make a one-day deposit under this rule immediately becomes a semi-weekly depositor for the rest of the calendar year and the following year.[14]

Federal Unemployment Taxes (FUTA)

How to determine your quarterly liability for FUTA: To determine your quarterly liability for FUTA, multiply the part of the first $7,000 of each employee's annual wages paid during the quarter by .006 (It used to be .008). If the resultant liability for all employees for the quarter is $100 or less, there is no requirement to deposit it immediately; you simply add it to your liability for the following quarter.

If your liability for any calendar quarter (plus any undeposited taxes for an earlier quarter) is more than $100, you are required to deposit the taxes by the end of the following month.

If the tax reported on your annual federal unemployment tax return Form 940, fewer deposits for the year:

- Is more than $100, you must deposit all of the tax by January 31st, or
- Is less than $100, you may pay the taxes when you file Form 940.

Electronic Federal Tax Payment System (EFTPS)

Under The Electronic Federal Tax Payment System (EFTPS) if your total deposits of Social Security, Medicare, Railroad Retirement and Income Taxes withheld were more than **$50,000** in your lookback period described above; you must make electronic deposits of all depository tax liabilities. Failure to do so will subject you to a penalty of 10% of the taxes due.

State Unemployment Taxes (SUTA)

Depending on your state of residence, additional unemployment taxes may be due to a State unemployment agency. You will normally pay a percentage of each employee's wages to a certain limit. The limit varies from State to State.

---

13 Ibid.

14 Accounting Setup For Startups, Slidesearchengine.com, http://www.slidesearchengine.com/slide/accounting-setup-for-startups/plus (accessed November 23, 2017).

The percentage for a new employer is higher than an existing employer with no claims. Your SUTA rate will fluctuate based on your experience — that is, the number of claims paid to former employees.

A good plan for hiring and terminating employees is very important. You can pay over $500 per year per employee or less than $25 per year per employee depending on how employees are terminated and how many unemployment claims are filed.

Default State Unemployment Rate for New Business for 2017

State	Standard 2017 New Employer Rate
Alabama	2.70%
Alaska	1.01 − 1.73%
Arizona	2.00%
Arkansas	3.20%
California	3.40%
Colorado	2.11%
Connecticut	3.90%
Delaware	1.70%
D.C.	2.70%
Florida	2.70%
Georgia	2.70%
Hawaii	2.40%
Idaho	1.40%
Illinois	3.45%
Indiana	1.6%, 2.5% or 3.23%
Iowa	1.00%
Kansas	2.70%
Kentucky	2.70%
Louisiana	1.23 − 3.07%
Maine	1.83%
Maryland	2.60%
Massachusetts	1.87%
Michigan	2.70%

Minnesota	1.44%
Mississippi	1.24 – 1.44%
Missouri	2.70%
Montana	1.18 – 2.68%
Nebraska	1.25%
Nevada	3.00%
New Hampshire	1.70%
New Jersey	2.80%
New Mexico	Greater of: 1.0% or Industry Average
New York	4.10%
North Carolina	1.00%
North Dakota	2.34%
Ohio	2.70%
Oklahoma	1.50%
Oregon	2.60%
Pennsylvania	3.68%
Puerto Rico	3.30%
Rhode Island	1.83%
South Carolina	1.39%
South Dakota	1.2% - 1st year 1.0% - 2nd & 3rd year
Tennessee	2.70%
Texas	2.70%
Utah	Industry Average
Vermont	1.00%
Virgin Islands	2.00%
Virginia	2.53%
Washington	Industry Average
West Virginia	2.70%
Wisconsin	3.05 – 4.55%
Wyoming	Industry Average

Supplemental Wages

Supplemental Wages are compensation paid in addition to an Employee's regular wages. They include, but are not limited to, bonuses, commissions, overtime pay, payments for accumulated sick leave, severance pay, awards, prizes, back pay and retroactive pay increases for current Employees, and payments for nondeductible moving expenses. Other payments subject to the supplemental wage rules include taxable Fringe Benefits and expense allowances paid under a non-accountable plan.[15]

How you withhold on supplemental payments depends on whether the supplemental payment is identified as a separate payment from regular wages.

Supplemental Wages combined with regular wages: If you pay Supplemental Wages with regular wages but do not specify the amount of each, withhold income tax as if the total were a single payment for a regular Payroll Period.

Supplemental Wages identified separately from regular wages: If you pay supplemental wages separately (or combine them in a single payment and specify the amount of each), the income tax withholding method depends partly on whether you withhold income tax from your Employee's regular wages:[16]

1. If you withheld income tax from an Employee's regular wages, you can use one of the following methods for the Supplemental Wages:

   - 1-a. Withhold a federal flat of 25% (no other percentage allowed).

   - 1-b. Add the supplemental and regular wages for the most recent payroll period this year. Then figure the income tax withholding as if the total was a single payment. Subtract the tax already withheld from the regular wages. Withhold the remaining tax from the Supplemental Wages.

2. If you did not withhold income tax from the Employee's regular wages, use method 1-b above.[17] (This would occur, for example, when the value of the Employee's withholding allowances claimed on Form W-4 is more than the wages.) Regardless of the method that you use to withhold income tax on Supplemental Wages, they are subject to Social Security, Medicare, and FUTA taxes.[18]

15 Compliance Connection | Federal Tax Calculations, https://adp-iat.adp.com/tools-and-resources/compliance-connection/federal-taxes/ (accessed November 4, 2017).

16 Publication 15: Circular E, Employer's Tax Guide; Chapter .., http://www.unclefed.com/IRS-Forms/2001/HTML/p1510.html (accessed November 5, 2017).

17 Ibid.

18 January 16, 2002 Memorandum, http://www.ncpublicschools.org/docs/fbs/resources/memos/withholdingrequirements. (accessed November 5, 2017).

State Supplemental Wage Tax Rates Table

State	Tax Rate
Alabama	5.0%
Arkansas	7.0%
California	6.0% 9.3% for stock options and bonuses
Colorado	4.63%
Georgia	Annual Wages: under $8,000 2.0% $8,000 -$10,000 3.0% $10,000 -$12,000 4.0% $12,000 -$15,000 5.0% over $15,000 6.0%
Idaho	7.8%
Illinois	3.0%
Indiana	3.4%
Iowa	6.0%
Kansas	5.0%
Maine	5.0%
Maryland	4.75% plus county rate
Michigan	4.0%; 3.9% eff. 7-1-04
Minnesota	6.25%
Missouri	6.0%
Montana	6.0%
Nebraska	6.25%
New Mexico	7.7%
New York	8.2%
North Carolina	6.0%
North Dakota	3.92%
Ohio	3.5%
Oklahoma	6.65%
Oregon	9.0%
Pennsylvania	3.07%
Rhode Island	7.0%
South Carolina	7.0%

Vermont	7.2%
West Virginia	Annual wages: under $10,000 3.0% $10,000 - $25,000 4.0% $25,000 - $40,000 4.5% $40,000 - $60,000 6.0% over $60,000 6.5%
	Annual wages: under $7,970 4.6% $ 7,970 - $15,590 6.15% $15,590 - $115,140 6.50% over $115,140 6.75%

Connecticut, Delaware, District of Columbia, Hawaii, Kentucky, Mississippi, New Jersey, and Virginia specify that Supplemental Wages be aggregated.

Tax regulations in Arizona, Louisiana, Massachusetts, and Utah do not contain provisions for a special supplemental tax rate.

Alaska, Florida, Nevada, New Hampshire, South Dakota, Tennessee, Texas, Washington, and Wyoming have no state income tax.

Fringe Benefits

A fringe benefit is a pay for performance in another way other than money. For example, providing a company car to the employee to commute back and forth to work. All fringe benefits are taxable and have to be included in the employee's pay unless excluded by law.

Gross income does not include fringe benefits that qualify for the exclusion, as described in the categories listed below. Fringe benefits that qualify for the exclusion are generally exempt from income tax and social security tax withholding (FICA and payment of federal unemployment tax (FUTA).[19]

Again, benefits that do not qualify are subject to those taxes.

No-Additional-Cost Service: This is a service provided to an employee that is excludable if the service is offered for sale to the public in the ordinary course of business and the employer does not incur a substantial additional cost.

For example, employers who furnish airline travel or hotel rooms to employees working in these businesses in such a way that the nonemployee customers are not displaced, and they incur no substantial additional cost in providing those services to the employees may exclude cost from the employee's gross income.[20]

Qualified Employee Discount: Any employee discount is an excludable qualified employee discount if:

1. In the case of property, it does not exceed the gross-profit percentage of the price that property is being offered to customers;

19 Accounting Setup For Startups, Slidesearchengine.com, http://www.slidesearchengine.com/slide/accounting-setup-for-startups/plus (accessed November 5, 2017).

20 Accounting Setup For Startups - Slideshare, https://www.slideshare.net/Incuba8/accounting-setup-for-startups (accessed November 5, 2017).

2. In the case of service, it does not exceed 20% of the price at which the service is being offered.

Working Condition Fringe: Any employer-provided property or service is an excludable benefit to the extent that they are deductible as ordinary and necessary business expenses had the employee paid for them. Under certain conditions, the fair market value of a qualified automobile demonstration used by a full-time auto salesperson is an excludable working condition fringe.

De Minimis Fringe: Property or services not otherwise tax-free are excludable if their value is so small as to make accounting unreasonable or administratively impractical. An operation of any eating facility for employees is an excludable de minimis fringe if it is located on or near the employer's business premises and the revenue derived normally equals or exceeds the direct operating costs of the facility.

Qualified Moving Expenses Reimbursement: An employee may exclude from gross income an amount received from an employer for payment of qualified moving expenses.

Transportation Fringe Benefits: Beginning in 1995, an employee may exclude from gross income certain maximum amounts received from an employer as reimbursements for transit passes, vanpooling expenses, and qualified parking expenses.[21]

New Hire Reporting

Mandatory new hire reporting is in place in all states. This reporting is designed to feed a national database for tracking down parents who are not making their child support payments.

It is mandatory in every state that every new hire is reported. Each state has slightly different requirements on timing and forms. Refer to IRS.gov for more information.

Other Tax Requirements

Whenever a wage payment is made, the employer must provide the employee with a statement of the gross wages and specific deductions (if any). Use the Form W-4 submitted by the employee and the tax tables provided in the employer's tax guides to determine the correct income tax to withhold.

If the employee fails to submit a Form W-4, the employer must withhold at the rate applicable to a single person who has no withholding exemptions. An employer must also complete a Form I-9 on each employee and obtain the necessary citizenship or other employment eligibility status verification. The employer must also furnish a Form W-2 to each employee showing remuneration and withheld taxes for each calendar year.

---

21 Payroll Taxes - Jkkr.com, http://www.jkkr.com/content/client/2a738ed4dac6a6818a3222c7d150bcde/uploads/5-bu (accessed November 5, 2017).

Flat rate expense account allowance, disability insurance paid by the employer, and moving expense reimbursements are among the items to be included as other compensation on a Form W-2. Upon request, a Form W-2 must be furnished to a terminated employee within 30 days after the request or the final wage payment, whichever is later.[22]

In all of the years I have been doing payroll for thousands of clients and hundreds of thousands of employees, I have never been asked to prepare a W-2 other than at year end. All other Form W-2s should be given to employees by January 31st of the following year.

The payroll tax requirements and the work related to compliance are quite cumbersome and complicated. Once a business is incorporated, and the owner must take compensation, or the business hires anyone, we recommend that a qualified payroll service is used. It has been our experience that the cost of the service far outweighs the personnel and management time required to operate the payroll system in the house.

Tax Rates

The following charts contain tax rates and the taxable wage basis for employers and employees. The limits and maximum contributions for 2018 given are per employee.[23]

FICA

- Employee Rate 6.20%
- On wages of $128,400.00

- Employer Rate 6.20%
- On wages of $128,400.00

Medicare

- Employee Rate 1.45%
- On wages of unlimited
- Employer Rate 1.45%

- On wages of unlimited
- Above wages of $200,000.00 for an individual or $250,000.00 for joint filers, there is a surcharge of 3.8%

Federal Unemployment

- Employer Rate 0.6% (After credit for paid SUI)
- On wages of $7,000.00

After collecting, depositing, creating returns and filing them, there are other things you need to be aware of when having employees. This is not an exclusive list by any means.

---

22 Accounting Setup For Startups - Slideshare, https://www.slideshare.net/Incuba8/accounting-setup-for-startups (accessed November 6, 2017).

23 https://www.ssa.gov/news/press/factsheets/colafacts2018.pdf

Documents: New employee documents that are required for every new employee include:

- Form W-4

- Form I-9

- Maybe the state equivalent of a W-4.

Form W-4: Form W-4 must be filled out by every newly hired employee. Have the employee fill it out, preferably on their first day but definitely before their first payroll is calculated. The W-4 gives you the information for the employee that you will need for the Form W-2 at the end of the year and the information to calculate their federal income tax withholding amounts.

If an employee tries to tell you a reason as to why you don't have to withhold from them, check with your CPA. There are a few people who will tell you they are not subject to withholding.

Except for full-time students working only part of a year, independent contractors and a few unusual exceptions the stories are just that, stories. If you have any questions, call your CPA or the IRS.

You are not responsible for the exemptions that an employee claims. If they claim more exemptions than they should the IRS will send you a "Lock-in Letter" telling you what to withhold from the employee's check and to ignore any Form W-4 that the employee presents to you.

If you don't follow the "Lock-in Letter", you are subject to penalties and interest on the uncollected amounts.

State Income Tax Withholding (if applicable): The State that your employee is in may require that you withhold State Income Tax. They may have their own form for calculating what that amount is to be or they may just use the Federal Form W-4. Again you can check that out with the State Department of Revenue or your CPA.

Form I-9: You must have each new employee fill out a Form I-9. *This is a Homeland Security form that proves the individual is authorized to work in the United States*. The employee fills out Section One. If the employee won't fill it out or provide the documents listed in Section two for you to review and hopefully copy, then you can't employ them.

You have until the third business day to fill out Section Two and examine the documents that the new employee provides, record which documents were provided and attest that the documents appear to be genuine. You are not required to copy the paper documents that the employee provides but I suggest that you do. It provides proof in the future that you did see them and they looked real.

There can be penalties including fines and prison time, for failing to comply with the law concerning authorized only people who have the legal authority to work in the United States.

You can't discriminate against anyone based on their national origin but if they don't have the required documents available for examination, don't employ them.

Employee Manual: Not required but very smart to have is a signature page from your employee handbook that shows that the employee has read and understands the handbook. It should also list the date of the handbook so you can know which version they signed. As you issue updates make sure, you get signatures on the updates as well.

By signing the signature page with the declaration that the employee has read and agrees on everything in the handbook the new employee has agreed to the terms of employment that you have set forth.

Every time you issue a change to the employee manual, you should have the employee certify that they either have seen, read and understood the change. You can also have them recertify that they have read and understood the entire handbook.

We'll go into the employee handbook in great detail later on in the Employee Handbook section.

Employment Application: You should have a signed employment application form from each employee. The employment application will list all of the employee's background and experience. It should include a space for them to list any criminal convictions. There should also be a specific statement that signing the application gives you the right to do a background check on them.

The application should state that any misstatements are grounds for immediate termination. Without a signed application, if you do find out that the employee was not truthful, the State Department of Labor may charge you back for unemployment claims because you can't "prove" the employee was less than forthcoming.

Retention of Employment Documents: Some of the data collected from the employee is required to be kept confidential. It is incumbent on the employer to protect this information from disclosure to unrelated or inappropriate parties.

The employer should set up a secure location for keeping this data protected. Secure them and restrict availability only to other employees who have to get the data to do their job.

- **How many years do you need to keep your employee files?** There are statutory numbers on some of the information. My suggestion is simple: never throw it away. I suggest at least ten full calendar years after the employee's termination date. Even then I would keep digital copies in a safe location for the foreseeable future.

Wages

Wages that are subject to tax generally include all payment you give to the employee in any form be it cash or kind. This includes sick pay, vacation pay, bonus pay, commissions and basically most everything paid to or for the employee while employed.

There are some exemptions to this. These are mostly fringe benefits that have been exempted by statute. See Publication 15-A for more information on wages and Publication 15-B about other compensation besides wages that may be taxable and certain fringe benefits, both taxable and non-taxable.

Other items you may come across that will or will not be taxable include: reimbursing employee expenses under accountable and nonaccountable plans;

- Per Diem,
- moving expenses,
- meals and lodging,
- health insurance,
- Health Savings Accounts (HSA),
- Medical Savings Accounts, and
- Flexible Spending Accounts.

Tips: If your employees receive tips there is a whole set of rules that apply to tips, wages of tipped employees, reporting tips, filing reports on tips, paying taxes on tips, tip credits and so on. Normally in the salon and spa business, all tips will normally be fully reportable and taxable as wages of the employees. Consult with your CPA.

Everything so far falls under Federal rules. If any of the States you operate in have State income tax withholding, the rules may be slightly different in calculating taxable wages for State Income Tax purposes. Refer to your state taxing authority for more information.

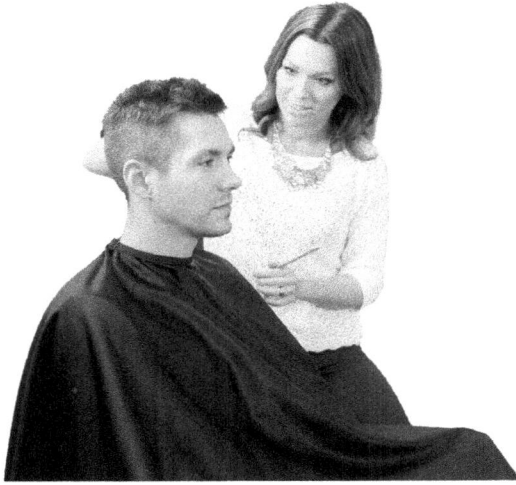

Paying Employees

Frequency: Pay frequency is left up to the States to regulate. It varies by:

- Each State,
- Classification of the employee,
- The amount they are paid, and
- Other factors.

No state allows, to our knowledge, payment less often than once a month.

We frequently find professionals paying themselves less often than once a month, but since it is themselves they are paying, who is going to complain?

Many States mandated a pay schedule of not less than twice a month for employees who qualify for overtime under the FLSA or referred to as non-exempt employees.

The most popular pay schedule we find among our client base is every two weeks, or bi-weekly (not semi-weekly that would be twice a week).

Almost no states mandate that weekly mandate payroll, (except New York for manual laborers) but you will need to check with your particular State.

Pay Statement: Pay Statement or Pay Stubs are required. Again, each State is different on what must be included in the statement. If you have a payroll processor, you won't have this problem. If you buy payroll software, you should be OK. If you just write checks, you need to know the details on what information you have to provide the employee each pay period. Some States will allow electronically and some States won't. However, you should be able to have electronic pay statements in your employee manual as a condition of employment.

Pay on Termination: When an employee is terminated when must you pay them? In California, you have to pay them that day. (A trick a California Administrative Judge taught us was don't terminate an employee, rather suspend them. Then on payday give them their check and terminate them. Good advice if your payroll office can't provide instantaneous checks). In other States, it varies.

Whether they quit or you fire them may make a difference in your State as well.

Fair Labor Standards Act (FLSA): The basic controlling Federal law concerning payroll and employment laws is the Fair Labor Standards Act of 1938 (FLSA), AKA as the Federal Wage-Hour Law. The FLSA covers:

- Federal minimum wage rate and Federal overtime rates to be paid to employees for work;Record keeping that is required of employers;
- Child labor restrictions, both amount, and type of work;
- Non-discriminating wages by gender for equal work.

Also, there are things that FLSA does not do:

- Require employers to offer paid time off (vacation, sick, jury duty, etc.);
- Require employers to offer paid holidays, breaks for lunch, smoking or coffee;
- Tell employers when they must pay employees;
- Control termination pay dates;
- Set the hours for Employees over the age of sixteen can work.

Other federal statutes or regulations may control some of these areas. However, most of the areas not covered by FLSA are handled by State statute.While FLSA does not control pay dates, the courts have ruled that wages not paid by the next regular payday date are in fact unpaid which violates other parts of the FLSA.

Every employer needs to understand not only FLSA but similar wage and hour statutes in the States that they operate in for two reasons:

1. Areas that the FLSA does not cover are most likely covered by State statutes or regulations.

2. In areas that are covered by the FLSA and the State wherever the State rules are more favorable to the employee, you must follow the State rules.

There are two ways that you can be subject as an employer to the FLSA; the first is what is called "**enterprise coverage**." All employees are covered by FLSA if:

1. A minimum of 2 employees are in jobs that relate to Interstate Commerce or are producing goods for Interstate Commerce; and

2. The business has gross sales exceeding $500,000 per year.

If you are simply an intrastate business; that is doing business only in one state, and not involved in producing products or services that cross state lines, you are not in interstate commerce and not subject to FSLA.

The Federal Department of Labor that enforces FLSA will do everything they can to try and make your business subject to FLSA. Certain businesses (and all their Employees) are specifically covered by the FLSA regardless of annual sales volume. They include:

- Hospitals

- Nursing homes

- Elementary and secondary schools and colleges (whether public or private)

- Public (government) agencies

The other way you become subject to FLSA is under the individual coverage test. An employee is covered by FLSA if the individual is engaged in Interstate Commerce. If the individual employee is involved in Interstate Commerce, then they are covered under FLSA regardless of whether the enterprise is covered or not.

Garnishments: Garnishments are one of the things that you have to deal with being in business. The requirements placed on you by the law vary from State to State. If you are using a payroll provider, they will take care of the garnishment and handle all the calculations and create the paychecks for you.

If you do your own payroll read the court order or letter very closely. *If you make a mistake, the person garnishing your employee or your employee may have an action against you.*

- **Voluntary**: Voluntary Garnishments are ones that the employee agrees to have placed as a lien on their wages. In some States, they are not allowed. Make sure you know your State law regarding voluntary garnishments.

- **Involuntary**: There are the Federal Mandated garnishments which include Child Support, Federal Taxes, and Guaranteed Student Loans. Even in States like Texas that doesn't allow creditor garnishments, you as an employer cannot avoid them.

With the State Attorney General's office handling child support on an involuntary basis, almost every company with more than a couple of employees is going to get hit with child support garnishments.

Student Loan defaults continue to grow, and many companies will see them as well. With the recession unpaid taxes increased and the IRS is beginning to start levying more of those cases.

Misclassification of Employees

Consequences of Treating an Employee as an Independent Contractor: If you classify an employee as an independent contractor and you have no reasonable basis for doing so, you may be held liable for employment taxes for that worker (the relief provisions, discussed below, will not apply). See Internal Revenue Code section 3509 for more information. The penalties are large and can be very severe.

Relief Provisions: If you have a reasonable basis for not treating a worker as an employee, you may be relieved from having to pay employment taxes for that worker. To get this relief, you must file all required federal information, returns on a basis consistent with your treatment of the worker. You (or your predecessor) must not have treated any worker holding a substantially similar position as an employee for any periods beginning after 1977. See Publication 1976, Section 530 Employment Tax Relief Requirements for more information.

Misclassified Workers Can File Social Security Tax Form: Workers who believe they have been improperly classified as independent contractors by an employer can use Form 8919, Uncollected Social Security and Medicare Tax on Wages to figure and report the employee's share of uncollected Social Security and Medicare taxes due on their compensation.[24]

Voluntary Classification Settlement Program: The Voluntary Classification Settlement Program (VCSP) is a new optional program that provides taxpayers with an opportunity to reclassify their workers as employees for future tax periods, for employment tax purposes with partial relief from federal employment taxes for eligible taxpayers that agree to prospectively treat their workers (or a class or group of workers) as employees.

To participate in this new voluntary program, the taxpayer must meet certain eligibility requirements, apply to participate in the VCSP by filing Form 8952, Application for Voluntary Classification Settlement Program, and enter into a closing agreement with the IRS.

---

24 Independent Contractor Self Employed Or Employee ..., https://www.irs.gov/businesses/small-businesses-self-employed/independent-contra (accessed November 6, 2017).

How is anyone going to know if you are misclassifying workers?

This is an easy situation to understand. If you have one person who thinks they should be paid as an employee instead of a contractor all they have to do is call or write a letter to your State Unemployment Department and you will be audited within a few weeks.

If a worker is fired and they go down to claim unemployment. The inability to find them on your State Unemployment filings will trigger an audit. An anonymous letter from a worker, a spouse, a family member, or increased anybody to the Unemployment Department will trigger an audit.

Periodically your business will be audited by your State Unemployment Department. They are funded by the US Department of Labor with your tax money. Their job, in part, is to make sure that all workers are classified properly. So it is not a matter of if you will be checked, but simply a matter of when.

Statutory and Non-Statutory Employees: If someone isn't an independent contractor then they are an employee. Actually, it is not that simple. Now we need to talk about statutory employees and statutory non-employees. The government has decided that some works will be employees regardless of what the determination would be under the common law test or any other test. These are called statutory employees.

The government has also decided that some workers will not be employees regardless again of how any determination tests would turn out. These are statutory non-employees.

Statutory Employees

Statutory Employees are employees who do not necessarily meet the common law test as an employee but have been deemed employees for Federal law purposes by the Federal government.

They are employees for employment tax purposes. Wages paid to statutory employees are not subject to income tax withholding on the Federal level. Wages are however subject to withholding for FICA purposes. In some instances, they will also be subject to Federal unemployment taxes as well.

There are four groups of statutory employees. They are:

1. **Agent-drivers or commission-drivers**: The worker must be working in the distribution of vegetables or fruit, meat, beverages other than milk, baked goods or in driving for a dry cleaning/laundry business. They also must be generating

income on a commission basis or on a difference in price between the sales price of the goods and the price that the drivers pays his employer for the goods. Many of your vending machine drivers are paid this way.

2. **Full-time life insurance salespersons**: The workers business activity must be principally marketing life insurance and/or annuity contracts. They do such work for just one insurance agency or company. The worker may have facilities include space, phone, computer systems and clerical staff along with marketing materials provided by the employer.

3. **Homeworkers**: The worker will work away from the employer's premises. They will work to specifications that the employer creates. They will work with material made available by the employer. The materials will be delivered per the employer's instructions. *The homeworker must make and be paid at least $100.00 in wages a calendar year before their earnings become taxable for FICA purposes.* The earnings of a home worker who does not qualify as an employee under the twenty common law rules are not subject to Federal Unemployment Tax. The homeworker definition does not mean a domestic worker that works in an employer's house.

4. **Traveling or city salespersons**: The salesperson must be a full-time worker. His or her main job has to be seeking orders from organizations who either are wholesaling in the products offered for resale or who use the products of the employer in their own establishments. A salesperson that casually sells orders for another employer can still be a Statutory Employee of the full-time employee only.

General requirements: Workers who qualify as one of the above types of workers have to meet the following conditions to qualify as a Statutory Employees.

1. They have to make sure that all the services will be performed by themselves personally.

2. They cannot have made a large investment in equipment or accommodations for the actual work.

3. There must be an ongoing relationship with the employer rather than a single time occurrence.

Statutory Non-Employees

Some types of workers that would clearly be employees under the twenty common law test are treated as independent contractors because Congress chose them to be independent contractors instead of employees. They are looked at by the IRS as independent contractors for income tax, FICA, and FUTA taxes, as long as clear circumstances are met.

There are two types:

Qualified real estate agents

This applies to sales people who are licensed by the appropriate licensing authority to operate as real estate agents in that State. Their duties would be performed in the process of the sale of real estate including showing prospective buyers properties and advertising properties for sale.

Direct Sellers

This applies to workers who sell consumer goods on a resale basis or for the commission. They normally sell in the client's home or possibly their own but not in an established retail sale location.

Think of Mary Kay or Fuller Brush (for the older generation) as examples. The exemption applies to newspaper delivery people or related products such as buying guides like the Greensheet. This also includes people who put on box shows for clothing companies.

General requirements: The two above non-employees must meet the following requirements before they are exempt from payroll tax withholding requirements.

1. Their compensation mainly has to depend on their sales or production and not on how long they work.

2. They must have a contract in writing agreeing that they will not be treated as an employee for Federal employment taxes.

There are several other considerations we need to take into account: Child Labor, Family Employees, Religious workers, interns.

Federal Child Labor Laws

FLSA (Fair Labor Standards Act) is the Federal Law that includes among many other things the Federal requirements concerning child labor. The FLSA's provision's concerning child labor are there to both protect their health, well-being and their educational opportunities.

A child is a natural person under the age of 18.

Minimum Age Other Than Agricultural Employment: The minimum age for employment outside of agriculture is 14 years of age. There are exceptions such as newspaper delivery; being a performer in radio, movie, television or stage productions. Also working for parents in the parent's owned non-agricultural business (except manufacturing or hazardous jobs).

Hours of Employment:

- Children aged 14 and 15 can work outside of school for a maximum of 3 hours per day and no more than 18 hours in a week during the school year.

- Children 14 and 15 can work a maximum of 8 hours a day on non-school days and 40 hours within a week on non-school weeks when school is not in session.

- Children 14 and 15 cannot go to work before 7 AM or work after 7 PM except the part of the year between June 1 st and Labor Day when they may work as late as 9 PM.

- Children aged 16 and 17 have no Federal restrictions on the number of hours they can work in a day or week.

Hazardous Employment: There are seventeen prohibited jobs for youth under the age of 18.[25] These include:

1. Manufacturing or storing explosives.

2. Driving a motorized vehicle or being an outside helper on a motor vehicle.

3. Mining coal.

4. Logging and/or working in a saw-milling.

5. Using power-driven woodworking machines.

6. Jobs that expose them to a radioactive source or to ionizing radiations.

7. Using powered hoist equipment.

8. Powered metal-forming, punching, or shearing machinery.

9. Mining other than coal.

10. Meat packing or processing (particularly, powered meat slicing machines).

11. Using powered bakery machinery.

12. Using powered paper products machinery.

13. Manufacturing brick, tile, and related products.

14. Powered circular saws, band saws, and guillotine shears.

15. Wrecking, demolition, and ship-breaking operations.

16. Roofing.

17. Excavation.

There are many industry-specific rulings and regulations regarding child labor. If you choose to employ anyone under the age of 18, I suggest you go to the US Department of Labor page on Child Labor and look through the various "Fact Sheet" for your industry.

25 What Is The Legal Working Age In Mount Pleasant, South .., https://answers.yahoo.com/question/index-?qid=20070825070652AAxfzQr (accessed November 6, 2017).

The States may have more restrictive Child Labor laws than the Federal restrictions. There is a list of the Child Labor Laws by State also on the DOL website. Make sure if you are hiring anybody under 18 that you check your State laws as well.

Volunteers: The Fair Labor Standards Act (FLSA) defines employment very broadly. The Supreme Court of the United States ruled, and the DOL has regulated in the case of individuals serving as unpaid volunteers in various community services. Individuals who volunteer or donate their services, usually on a part-time basis, for public service employees, and without contemplation, religious or humanitarian objectives, without pay, are not considered employees of the religious, charitable or similar non-profit organizations that receive their service.[26]

Members of civic organizations may help at shelter workrooms or may send members or students into hospice, hospitals, nursing facilities, assisted living homes and the like to provide personal services for the infirm or elderly.

Parents of students may volunteer in a school library or lunch room as a civic activity to help keep up standards of services for their children, they may volunteer to chaperone or to drive a school vehicle for a drama camp or band trip.

In the same vein, people may volunteer to do things like driving, helping with a blood drive for the local blood bank, mentoring underserved, acting as counselors, Scoutmaster and so on.

Under FLSA workers cannot volunteer services to for-profit private sector employers. However, normally individuals can volunteer services to public sector employers.

In 1985 the amendments to the FLSA were clear that individuals were allowed to volunteer their services to public agencies or within their community, except, public sector employers may not allow or require their employees to do the same work for pay and as a volunteer as well.

There is no prohibition on employees in private businesses from volunteering in any way in the public employment sector of the economy.

Interns: Interns in the "for-profit" business sector of the economy who are classified as employees are subject to FLSA and State minimum wage and overtime standards like any other employee.

There can be situations where individuals who work in "for-profit" business sector internships or training programs that may not be paid to do so. The Supreme Court definition of "suffer or permit to work" should not be held so as to make an individual who works for their own education an employee under certain circumstances.

26 Elaws - Employment Laws Assistance For Workers And Small .., https://webapps.dol.gov/elaws/whd/flsa/docs/volunteers.asp (accessed November 7, 2017).

These six principles must be looked at when making this decision:

1. The intern who is actually performing work, the work is the equivalent of the same training that would be given in an educational setting.

2. The experience the intern receives accrues to the benefit of the individual intern.

3. The individual intern is not used to replace other workers; the intern works under the close direction of current employees.

4. The employer that employees the intern receive no apparent current return from the work of the intern, and in fact may cause the employer additional costs or reduced efficiency.

5. The individual is not promised a position at the end of the internship.

6. The employer and the individual intern have a mutual understanding that there is no compensation for the labor or time expended by the intern.

If all of the criteria are in place, then an employer-employee bond is not forged under the FLSA and standards in place for overtime, and minimum wages do not apply. This exclusion is designed to be very restrictive and hard to meet. It has been tested in the courts recently and a number of the decisions have been in favor of the interns being employees and not unpaid interns, particularly for overtime.

Basically the more an internship is structured around an academic experience rather than an employer's actual operations, the more likely it is to survive as an unpaid internship.

The broader the applicability of the skills learned the more likely the internship would be viewed as education, as opposed to skills only applicable to the employer. The fact that the work assists the employer does not disqualify the work because as well as benefiting the employer it is providing new skill sets or better working habits to the intern.

If the employer would have had to hire additional employees if the interns were not there to do the work the internship will not survive scrutiny to remain as excluded from FLSA. Neither will it if the intern is used to replace workers that were there. Also, it is expected that the intern would need more supervision than a standard worker, otherwise it suggests work, not training.

If an individual is placed with an employer as an unpaid intern for a probationary period with the justifiable expectation that they would then be placed in a permanent position the intern would be viewed as an employee under FLSA, not as an unpaid intern.

You as an Employee

If you work for yourself are you an employee? Maybe?

- If you have incorporated your business and worked in it, then you are an employee.

- If you are not incorporated, and you work in your own business you are a sole proprietor; you are not an employee.

- If you are in a partnership with your wife you may or may not be employees. If you and your wife are in a qualified joint venture, and you two are the only members of the joint event, and you elect to be treated as a partnership for Federal Tax purposes you are not employees.

  Before you do that make sure you have a good CPA because it is probably not a wise tax move for the two of you. If the two of you work in a corporation, regardless of the actual ownership you are employees.

In either case of the corporation, there is a concern with how much of the earnings are compensation as an employee and how much of the earnings are distributions to the owners as investors and therefore, not subject to employment tax. That is a topic for a different chapter.

Independent Contractor Sample Contract

Here is a sample of an independent contractors contract. It lays out obligations and responsibilities on both sides of the agreement. Something like this is a good idea just to make sure you don't end up in court without something to use as a shield against an upset ex-contractor.

INDEPENDENT CONTRACTOR AGREEMENT

(Company)

This Independent Contractor Agreement ("Agreement") is entered into as of

_____, _____, by and between _____, with a

principal place of business at _____ ("Company"), and

_____, a _____ corporation, with a principal place of business at

_____ ("Contractor").[27]

1. Services.

1.1 Nature of Services.

The contractor will perform the services, as more particularly described in Exhibit A, for Company as an Independent Contractor (the "Services").

The Services have been specially ordered and commissioned by Company. To the extent the Services include materials subject to copyright; Contractor agrees that the Services are done as "work made for hire" as that term is defined under U.S. copyright law and that as a result, the company will own all copyrights in the Services.

The contractor will perform such services in a diligent and workmanlike manner and in accordance with the schedule, if any, set forth in Exhibit A. The content, style, form, and format of any work product of the Services shall be completely satisfactory to Company and shall be consistent with Company's standards.[28] Except as specified in Exhibit A, Company agrees that Contractor's services need not be rendered at any specific location and may be rendered at any location selected by Contractor. Contractor hereby grants Company the right, but not the obligation, to use and to license others the right to use Contractor, and Contractor's employees', name, voice, signature, photograph, likeness and biographical information in connection with and related to the Services.

27 Independent Contractor Agreement 1 - Anyform.org, http://anyform.org/doc/14563/independent-contractor-agreement-1 (accessed November 7, 2017).

28 Independent Contractor Agreement - Chapman University, https://www.chapman.edu/research/institutes-and-centers/leatherby-center/_files/ (accessed November 7, 2017).

1.2 Relationship of the Parties.

Contractor enters into this Agreement as and shall continue to be, an Independent Contractor. All Services shall be performed only by Contractor and Contractor's employees. Under no circumstances shall Contractor, or any of Contractor's employees, look to Company as his/her employer, or as a partner, agent or principal.

Neither Contractor nor any of Contractor's employees, shall be entitled to any benefits accorded to Company's employees, including without limitation worker's compensation, disability insurance, vacation or sick pay. Contractor shall be responsible for providing, at Contractor's expense, and in Contractor's name, unemployment, disability, worker's compensation and other insurance, as well as licenses and permits usual or necessary for conducting the Services.

1.3 Compensation and Reimbursement.

Contractor shall be compensated and reimbursed for the Services as set forth on Exhibit B. Completeness of work product shall be determined by Company in its sole discretion, and Contractor agrees to make all revisions, additions, deletions or alterations as requested by Company. No other fees and/or expenses will be paid to Contractor unless such fees and/or expenses have been approved in advance by the appropriate Company executive in writing.

Contractor shall be solely responsible for any and all taxes, Social Security contributions or payments, disability insurance, unemployment taxes, and other payroll-type taxes applicable to such compensation. Contractor hereby indemnifies and holds Company harmless from, any claims, losses, costs, fees, liabilities, damages or injuries suffered by Company arising out of Contractor's failure with respect to its obligations in this Section 1.3.[29]

1.4 Personnel.

Contractor represents and warrants to Company that its employees performing Services hereunder will have (a) sufficient expertise, training and experience to accomplish the Services; and (b) executed agreements which state that (i) all work done by the employee will be a work made for hire, as that term is defined under U.S. copyright law, and will be owned by Contractor; and (ii) the employee assigns all rights in and to all work done by the employee to Contractor. Contractor agrees that all its personnel shall be compensated, taxes withheld, and other benefits made available as required by applicable law and regulations.

---

29 Independent Contractor Agreement - Tidyform, https://www.tidyform.com/download/file/independent-contractor-agreement-1/pdf (accessed November 7, 2017).

Contractor shall require all employees who perform Services and/or have performed Services hereunder to sign a copy of the form attached hereto as Exhibit C and Contractor shall forward copies of all of such forms to Company within five (5) days of executing the Agreement and/or within five (5) days of assigning a new employee to perform Services hereunder.[30]

2. Protection of Company's Confidential Information.

2.1 Confidential Information.

The company now owns and will hereafter develop, compile and own certain proprietary techniques, trade secrets, and confidential information which have great value in its business (collectively, "Company Information").[31]

The company will be disclosing Company Information to Contractor during Contractor's performance of the Services. Company Information includes not only information disclosed by Company, but also information developed or learned by Contractor during Contractor's performance of the Services.

Company information is to be broadly defined and includes all information which has or could have commercial value or other utility in the business in which Company is engaged or contemplates engaging or the unauthorized disclosure of which could be detrimental to the interests of Company, whether or not such information is identified by Company.

By way of example and without limitation, Company Information includes any and all information concerning discoveries, developments, designs, improvements, inventions, formulas, software programs, processes, techniques, know-how, data, research techniques, customer and supplier lists, marketing, sales or other financial or business information, scripts, and all derivatives, improvements and enhancements to any of the above. Company Information also includes like third-party information which is in Company's possession under an obligation of confidential treatment.

2.2 Protection of Company Information.

Contractor agrees that at all times during or subsequent to the performance of the Services, Contractor will keep confidential and not divulge, communicate, or use Company Information, except for Contractor's own use during the Term of this Agreement to the extent necessary to perform the Services.[32]

30 Independent Contractor Agreement 1 - Anyform.org, http://anyform.org/doc/14563/independent-contractor-agreement-1 (accessed November 7, 2017).

31 Independent Contractor Agreement - Chapman University, https://www.chapman.edu/research/institutes-and-centers/leatherby-center/_files/ (accessed November 7, 2017).

32 Independent Contractor Agreement - Tidyform, https://www.tidyform.com/download/file/independent-contractor-agreement-1/pdf (accessed November 7, 2017).

Contractor further agrees not to cause the transmission, removal or transport of tangible embodiments of, or electronic files containing, Company Information from Company's principal place of business, without prior written approval of Company.[33]

2.3 Exceptions.

Contractor's obligations with respect to any portion of the Company Information as set forth above shall not apply when Contractor can document that (i) it was in the public domain at the time it was communicated to Contractor by Company; (ii) it entered the public domain subsequent to the time it was communicated to Contractor by Company through no fault of Contractor; (iii) it was in Contractor's possession free of any obligation of confidence at the time it was communicated to Contractor by Company; or (iv) it was rightfully communicated to Contractor free of any obligation of confidence subsequent to the time it was communicated to Contractor by Company.

2.4 Company Property.

All materials, including without limitation documents, drawings, drafts, notes, designs, computer media, electronic files and lists, including all additions to, deletions from, alterations of, and revisions in the foregoing (together the "Materials"), which are furnished to Contractor by Company or which are developed in the process of performing the Services, or embody or relate to the Services, the Company Information or the Innovations (as defined below), are the property of Company, and shall be returned by Contractor to Company promptly at Company's request together with any copies thereof, and in any event promptly upon expiration or termination of this Agreement for any reason.

Contractor is granted no rights in or to such Materials, the Company Information or the Innovations, except as necessary to fulfill its obligations under this Agreement. Contractor shall not use or disclose the Materials, Company Information or Innovations to any third party.[34]

3. Prior Knowledge and Relationships.

3.1 Prior Inventions and Innovations.

The contractor has disclosed on Exhibit D, a complete list of all inventions or innovations made by Contractor prior to the commencement of the Services for Company and which Contractor desires to exclude from the application of this Agreement. The contractor will disclose to Company such additional information as Company may request regarding such inventions or innovations to enable Company to assess their

33 Ibid.
34 Independent Contractor Agreement - Tidyform, https://www.tidyform.com/download/file/independent-contractor-agreement-1/pdf (accessed November 7, 2017).

extent and significance. Company agrees to receive and hold all such disclosures in confidence.[35]

3.2 Other Commitments.

Except as disclosed on Exhibit D to this Agreement, Contractor has no other agreements, relationships or commitments to any other person or entity which conflict with Contractor's obligations to Company under this Agreement. Contractor agrees not to enter into any agreement, either written or oral, in conflict with this Agreement.

4. Assignment of Contractor's Inventions and Copyrights.

4.1 Disclosure.

Contractor will promptly disclose in writing to Company all works, products, discoveries, developments, designs, innovations, improvements, inventions, formulas, processes, techniques, know-how and data (whether or not patentable, and whether or not at a commercial stage, or registrable under copyright or similar statutes) which are authored, made, conceived, reduced to practice or learned by Contractor (either alone or jointly with others) during the period Contractor provides the Services as a result of performing the Services including any concepts, ideas, suggestions and approaches related thereto or contained therein (collectively, the "Innovations").[36]

4.2 Assignment.

Contractor hereby assigns and agrees to assign to Company, without royalty or any other consideration except as expressly set forth herein, all worldwide right, title and interest Contractor may have or acquire in and to (i) all Materials; (ii) all Innovations (iii) all worldwide patents, patent applications, copyrights, mask work rights, trade secrets rights and other intellectual property rights in any Innovations; and (iv) any and all "moral rights" or right of "droit moral" (collectively "Moral Rights"), that Contractor may have in or with respect to any Innovations.

To the extent any Moral Rights are not assignable, Contractor waives, disclaims and agrees that Contractor will not enforce such Moral Rights.[37]

Contractor agrees that such assignment shall extend to all languages and include the right to make translations of the Materials and Innovations. Additionally, Contractor agrees, at no charge to Company, but at Company's sole expense, to sign and deliver to Company (either during or subsequent to Contractor's performance of the Services) such documents as Company considers desirable to evidence the

35 Independent Contractor Agreement 1 - Anyform.org, http://anyform.org/doc/14563/independent-contractor-agreement-1 (accessed November 7, 2017).

36 Independent Contractor Agreement 1 - Anyform.org, http://anyform.org/doc/14563/independent-contractor-agreement-1 (accessed November 7, 2017).

37 Ibid.

assignment of all rights of Contractor, if any, described above to Company and Company's ownership of such rights and to do any lawful act and to sign and deliver to Company any document necessary to apply for, register, prosecute or enforce any patent, copyright or other right or protection relating to any Innovations in any country of the world.[38]

4.3 Power of Attorney.

Contractor hereby irrevocably designates and appoints each of Company and its Secretary as Contractor's agent and attorney-in-fact, to act for and on Contractor's behalf and stead, for the limited purpose of executing and filing any such document and doing all other lawfully permitted acts to further the prosecution, issuance and enforcement of patents, copyrights or other protections which employ or are based on Innovations with the same force and effect as if executed and delivered by Contractor.

4.4 Representations and Warranties.

Contractor represents and warrants to Company that (a) Contractor has full power and authority to enter into this Agreement including all rights necessary to make the foregoing assignments to Company; that in performing under the Agreement; (b) Contractor will not violate the terms of any agreement with any third party; and (c) the Services and any work product thereof are the original work of Contractor, do not and will not infringe upon, violate or misappropriate any patent, copyright, trade secret, trademark, contract, or any other publicity right, privacy right, or proprietary right of any third party.[39]

Contractor shall defend, indemnify and hold Company and its successors, assigns and licensees harmless from any and all claims, actions and proceedings, and the resulting losses, damages, costs, and expenses (including reasonable attorney's fees) arising from any claim, action or proceeding based upon or in any way related to Contractor's or Contractor's employees, breach or alleged breach of any representation, warranty or covenant in this Agreement, and/or from the acts or omissions of Contractor or Contractor's employees.

5. Termination of Agreement.

5.1 Term.

This Agreement shall be effective from the date first listed above for the period set forth in Exhibit A, or until completion of the Services, as applicable, unless sooner terminated by either party in accordance with the terms and conditions of this

---

38 Independent Contractor Agreement 1 - Anyform.org, http://anyform.org/doc/14563/independent-contractor-agreement-1 (accessed November 8, 2017).

39 Independent Contractor Agreement - Tidyform, https://www.tidyform.com/download/file/independent-contractor-agreement-1/pdf (accessed November 8, 2017).

Agreement ("Term"). This Agreement is terminable by either party at any time, with or without cause, effective upon notice to the other party.

If Company exercises its right to terminate the Agreement, any obligation it may otherwise have under this Agreement shall cease immediately, except that Company shall be obligated to compensate Contractor for work performed up to the time of termination. If Contractor exercises its right to terminate the Agreement, any obligation it may otherwise have under this Agreement shall cease immediately.

Additionally, this Agreement shall automatically terminate upon Contractor's death. In such event, Company shall be obligated to pay Contractor's estate or beneficiaries only the accrued but unpaid compensation and expenses due as of the date of death.

5.2 Continuing Obligations of Contractor.

The provisions of Sections 1.1 (as relates to creation and ownership of copyright), 1.2, 1.3, 2, 3, 4, 5.2, and 6 shall survive expiration or termination of this Agreement for any reason. [40]

6. Additional Provisions.

6.1 Governing Law and Attorney's Fees.

This Agreement shall be governed by and construed in accordance with the laws of the State of California, without regard to its choice of law principles. The parties consent to exclusive jurisdiction and venue in the federal and state courts sitting in Orange County, California.

In any action or suit to enforce any right or remedy under this Agreement or to interpret any provision of this Agreement, the prevailing party shall be entitled to recover its reasonable attorney's fees, costs, and other expenses.

6.2 Binding Effect.

This Agreement shall be binding upon, and inure to the benefit of, the successors, executors, heirs, representatives, administrators and permitted assigns of the parties hereto. Contractor shall have no right to (a) assign this Agreement, by operation of law or otherwise; or (b) subcontract or otherwise delegate the performance of the Services without Company's prior written consent which may be withheld as Company determines in its sole discretion. Any such purported assignment shall be void. [41]

---

40 Independent Contractor Agreement 1 - Anyform.org, http://anyform.org/doc/14563/independent-contractor-agreement-1 (accessed November 8, 2017).

41 Ibid.

6.3 Severability.

If any provision of this Agreement shall be found invalid or unenforceable, the remainder of this Agreement shall be interpreted so as for best to reasonably effect the intent of the parties.

6.4 Entire Agreement.

This Agreement, including the Exhibits, constitutes the entire understanding and agreement between the parties with respect to its subject matter and supersedes all prior and contemporaneous agreements or understandings, inducements or conditions, express or implied, written or oral, between the parties.

6.5 Injunctive Relief.

Contractor acknowledges and agrees that in the event of a breach or threatened breach of this Agreement by Contractor, Company will suffer irreparable harm and will, therefore, be entitled to injunctive relief to enforce this Agreement.[42]

6.6 Contractor's Remedy.

Contractor's remedy, if any, for any breach of this Agreement shall be solely for damages and Contractor shall look solely to Company for recovery of such damages. Contractor waives and relinquishes any right Contractor may otherwise have to obtain injunctive or equitable relief against any third party with respect to any dispute arising under this Agreement. Contractor shall look solely to Company for any compensation which may be due to Contractor hereunder.

6.7 Agency.

The contractor is not Company's agent or representative and has no authority to bind or commit Company to any agreements or other obligations.

6.8 Amendment and Waivers.

Any term or provision of this Agreement may be amended, and the observance of any term of this Agreement may be waived, only by a writing signed by the party to be bound. The waiver by a party of any breach or default in performance shall not be deemed to constitute a waiver of any other or succeeding breach or default.[43]

The failure of any party to enforce any of the provisions hereof shall not be construed to be a waiver of the right of such party thereafter to enforce such provisions.

42 Independent Contractor Agreement 1 - Anyform.org, http://anyform.org/doc/14563/independent-contractor-agreement-1 (accessed November 8, 2017).
43 Ibid.

6.9 Time.

Contractor agrees that time is of the essence in this Agreement.

6.10 Notices.

Any notice, demand, or request with respect to this Agreement shall be in writing and shall be effective only if it is delivered by personal service, by air courier with receipt of delivery, or mailed, certified mail, return receipt requested, postage prepaid, to the address set forth above.

Such communications shall be effective when they are received by the addressee; but if sent by certified mail in the manner set forth above, they shall be effective five (5) days after being deposited in the mail. Any party may change its address for such communications by giving notice to the other party in conformity with this section.

CAUTION: THIS AGREEMENT AFFECTS YOUR RIGHTS TO INNOVATIONS YOU MAKE PERFORMING YOUR SERVICES, AND RESTRICTS YOUR RIGHT TO DISCLOSE OR USE COMPANY'S CONFIDENTIAL INFORMATION DURING OR SUBSEQUENT TO YOUR SERVICES. CONTRACTOR HAS READ THIS AGREEMENT CAREFULLY AND UNDERSTANDS ITS TERMS. CONTRACTOR HAS COMPLETELY FILLED OUT EXHIBIT D TO THIS AGREEMENT.[44]

Contractor company

By: _____

CONTRACTOR (Print Name) _____

SIGNATURE OF CONTRACTOR _____

DATE _____

Forms mentioned in this section:

IRS Form W4

IRS Form 1099

IRS Form 1096

Circular E, Publication 15, Employer's Tax Guide

The Electronic Federal Tax Payment System (EFTPS)

Form I-9

Publication 15-A

Publication 15-B

Form 8952, Application for Voluntary Classification Settlement Program

---

44 Independent Contractor Agreement - Tidyform, https://www.tidyform.com/download/file/independent-contractor-agreement-1/pdf (accessed November 8, 2017).

She quit and filed for unemployment.

How to avoid unemployment claims.

What Causes an Unemployment Claim?

An ex-employee goes to the State unemployment office and files a claim for unemployment benefits. The office representative takes the information and helps the ex-employee file a claim for benefits and automatically attempts to charge the cost of the claim against you the employer. **If they are successful in charging your company, it will raise your unemployment tax rate for several years as the State tries to recoup the total that is paid out to the employee.**

One unemployment claim can get very expensive running into the thousands of dollars. Unemployment benefits vary by State. The higher they are in your State, the more you will pay in additional unemployment taxes to cover the benefits paid.

Understand the **unemployment department in your State is not your friend** when it comes to unemployment. Getting benefits for the unemployed is their task. That is their reason for existence. As in any bureaucracy the more headcount, the more the bosses get paid, and the safer everyone is at keeping their job. If they actively were on the side of the employer and denying as many cases as they could, they would be putting their jobs in jeopardy.

One thing about an unemployment claim is the longer an employee works for you up to a limit of close to two years the more the claim will be. So if you have to terminate someone without cause do it as quickly into their employment as you can. It will save you money, grief, and heartache!

To avoid unemployment claims, you must learn how to terminate employees properly.

What Should You Do if an Employee Quits?

Document. Document. Document. If an employee quits make sure to document it. You can offer them a letter of voluntary termination when they pick up their last check. You can't withhold the check if they don't want to sign the letter but you can urge them to sign it before moving on to whatever future they are going to. You get more flies with honey, so the nicer you are at termination, you may get them to sign it without issue. Only you will know that it is proof that they quit and will help your cause if they decide to file for unemployment.

If they don't sign a letter of termination or provide you with something in writing, take the extra step to document the circumstances. Take statements from co-workers, put them in writing, have them signed and dated by the employee and a witness, as timely as possible.

Don't get upset or be nasty with a terminating employee no matter how much you might feel that they have taken advantage of you. It is their privilege to quit as it was yours to hire them. Hard feelings may turn into vindictiveness.

If they quit in a huff still try at the point, they pick up the last check try to get a written agreement of voluntary termination. If they refuse, document all the circumstances. Get statements and witnesses. You'll be glad you did.

If they don't show up to pick up their last check, make sure you send a certified letter. In the letter state that as far as you can determine, they have voluntarily terminated their position by not returning to your workplace. Send it to their last known address. If the letter is returned save it in their file as well. Don't tear up the check. That money is no longer yours even if they never pick up their check.

If they send an email or letter quitting keep it safe in your personnel files. That is your proof that they quit if they decide to file an unemployment claim anyway.

Again...Document. Document everything. **It may be worth thousands of dollars to you.** Remember if you have to fight a claim **provable facts are the best defense**.

What Should You Do if You Terminate an Employee?

You **can** terminate an employee for cause! If you have cause under the law of your State, the claim will either not be paid, or if paid will not be charged back to you the employer.

What is cause?

Cause is ultimately what the Court says is cause. There are many lists, and some are wrong:

Here is a list of cause to terminate an employee from The Hartford:

1. Incompetence, including lack of productivity or poor quality of work.

2. Insubordination and related issues such as dishonesty and breaking company rules.

3. Attendance issues, such as frequent absences or chronic tardiness.

4. Theft or other criminal behavior including revealing trade secrets.

5. Sexual harassment and other discriminatory behavior in the workplace.

6. Physical violence or threats against other employees.[45]

---

45 Acceptable Reasons For Termination - The Hartford, https://www.thehartford.com/business-playbook/in-depth/valid-reasons-fire-employ (accessed November 8, 2017).

What do you think about that list? Sounds right, right? Maybe not.

Number one lists incompetence as a cause for termination.

Most State Unemployment Departments will say in response to a claim incompetence: "Then why did you hire them in the first place and deny cause."

The rest of number one talks about production or quality of work. What are the standards you have set in your employee manual? If you don't have an employee manual, there are no standards for performance, and there is no cause for firing the employee. Sounds harsh, sure. But I say again the State Unemployment Department is not your friend. In this day and age, an employee handbook/policy manual is a requirement for your financial protection.

Number two and three are also ones that require a policy manual. If the rules are not written down then as far as the State Unemployment Department is concerned, they don't exist. If the employee is not aware of the rules how can he know he is breaking them. You can make reasonable rules for attendance and tardiness in your employee manual.

Number four. Theft is normally considered cause. But you have to prove it. If you catch an employee stealing and fire them, that is not stealing as far as the State Unemployment Department is concerned. You better have the arrest record and the conviction in a court. Otherwise, it is only hearsay and won't be recognized as cause.

If you want to let him off the legal hook, make the employee write out preferably in long hand a full confession of the theft. Have it witnessed by an outside third party as well as yourself. It may hold up. Revealing trade secrets is just another form of theft.

Worse than that you can't talk about the employee being a thief if you don't have the conviction for theft. I have seen companies of giving a reference saying that an employee was fired being successfully sued by the fired employee for slander and defamation of character. Yes, it happens.

Number five. Sexual harassment or discrimination. Again you have to define it to enforce it.

Number six. Violence and threats. Sounds easy enough to fire for cause. To be on the safe side, you should have an explanation of it in detail in your employee manual. What does that mean? You will then have to fire everybody involved in a fight. Even if someone is attacked without provocation and defends themselves. You have to fire everybody involved. Not fair but necessary. If not you will get sued by some lawyer looking to make a quick buck and will probably lose because you took it upon yourself to judge the actions.

The Hartford has made a good start here but as you can see **cause is only what you can prove.** If you have not previously defined it, then you probably can't prove cause. You may well have to prove it to an administrative law judge that works for the State Unemployment Department. Again they are not your friend.

Make rules that are followable.

Don't make ridiculous rules and fire someone for cause because they did not follow them or you will probably lose that case as well.

There has to be a business reason behind your rules, and they also cannot discriminate based on race, gender, religion, national origin, physical or mental disability, age, sexual orientation, and gender identity. The discrimination cannot be deliberate or unintended, and the judge is the one who decides on discrimination and reasonableness. If there is not some verifiable business-based reason that all your employees are bald, then you can't mandate it. Make sure you can provide it if it is a reasonable demand.

There is an Unemployment Case Filed Against You, What Now?

Is it documented? If not start immediately to gather all potential documentation concerning the termination and its reasons.

Answer the first document from your State Unemployment Department. **Answer any request from them.** Failing to answer one of them may give the case to the employee and could forestall you from winning the case.

On the first document, you need to answer with what the crux of your defense will be, but you don't have to present all of your evidence. If you fired them for cause say so and what the cause was. You don't have to present everything. Sometimes the employee will get discouraged with the first rejection and move on. Probably not though as the Unemployment Department stands ready to show them how to appeal.

If the employee appeals and there is going to be a hearing, this is when you need to put your total package together and send it to the hearing office. Have it in a logical order. **Send a copy not the originals.**

Mark the documents so in the hearing, you can refer a particular document to the hearing officer quickly and easily.

Present a copy to the ex-employee in the same package if you are required. If you want to be tricky, don't mark the documents in the package for the ex-employee to make it harder for the ex-employee to reference. If called on it in court simply say, "it was just an oversight, all the documents are there."

Appeal and appeal until the end of the process. **If either one of you does not show up for a hearing or answer a communication (with good cause), you lose.** Make the ex-employee be the loser. Save yourself the money. Win.

You Want to Fire an Employee But Don't Have Cause

It's your business: Why can't you simply fire employees as you see fit?

There are at least 90,000 reasons why that's not a good idea. That's the number of charges against employers for unfair termination received by the Equal Employment Opportunity Commission (EEOC) in 2016.

Even if the issue, in your eyes, is obvious incompetence or persistently obnoxious behavior, the employee can always file a complaint claiming discrimination based on race, sex, religion, age, or political beliefs.[46]

So what do you do?

1. You can just fire them and take the hit for the unemployment chargeback.

2. You can start documenting a case for cause. Of course, this is the one we would choose.

---

46 Acceptable Reasons For Termination - The Hartford, https://www.thehartford.com/business-playbook/in-depth/valid-reasons-fire-employ (accessed November 8, 2017).

Obviously, (I hope) you want to get rid of this employee because they are not doing a good job for you. Document the failures. Counsel the employee on where they need to improve to the standards of the company and show them where they are not meeting that standard. Improve your employee handbook to establish your cause.

Document, document, document. When you do terminate an employee, it should be no surprise. You should have multiple written warnings in the file. You should be comfortable that you can prove cause to a hearing office. Then if the employee has not taken the hint that they need to find a different job, you can pull the trigger and fire them.

Reading this chapter has probably made you realize that the best thing you can do is to increase your emphasis on hiring the right person for the job. That is a correct assumption but people and times change, and you need to be ready for the good of your business to be able to fire people, hopefully without paying an unemployment claim. But not firing the vexatious employee may not be a mistake, even if you have to pay for it. Know your options.

Unemployment Claims That May Be Non-Chargeable

There are certain claims that are made by ex-employees that will be paid but are not chargeable back to the employer if you did not employ them in the "Chargeable" time.

The State looks back to a period and considers those employers in that period, and if the employee worked for you in that period but left voluntarily or terminated for cause, you should not be charged back for the cost of the benefits paid. If your employment of the ex-employee was not during the chargeable period, then you won't be charged.

Once I had an employee who could no longer work for my company due to medical reasons. He technically became unemployable. He received unemployment benefits because he was terminated because he could not return to work. But we were not charged because of the medical reasons not allowing him to return. It was cause for us even though it was not something he did voluntarily. In Texas, we were not charged-back, but he received unemployment benefits.

Employment Laws by State

Know your State unemployment and labor laws. View this link and find your State for more information. While it is "dry" reading, it's important for you and your business to know them well.

http://www.employmentlawhandbook.com/state-employment-and-labor-laws/

Additional Information:
Selected Supreme Court Decisions

The Supreme Court in **Phillips v. Martin Marietta Corp**. holds that Title VII prohibition against sex discrimination means that employers cannot discriminate on the basis of sex plus other factors such as having school-age children. In practical terms, EEOC›s policy forbids employers from using one hiring policy for women with small children and a different policy for males with children of a similar age.

In **Espinoza v. Farah Manufacturing Co**., the Supreme Court holds that non-citizens are entitled to Title VII protection and states that a citizenship requirement may violate Title VII if it has the purpose or effect of discriminating on the basis of national origin. [47]

In **Albermarle Paper Co. v. Moody**, the Supreme Court decides that after a court has found an employer guilty of discrimination, the "wronged" employee is presumed to be entitled to back pay.

The Supreme Court in **Trans World Airlines, Inc. v. Hardison** decides its first Title VII religious discrimination case. The Court states that under Title VII employers must reasonably accommodate an employee›s religious needs unless to do so would create an undue hardship for the employer. The Court defines hardship as anything more than de minimis cost. [48]

In **Los Angeles Department of Water and Power v. Manhart**, the Supreme Court rules that an employer may not use the fact that women as a group live longer than men to justify a policy of requiring women employees to make larger contributions than men to a pension plan to receive the same monthly pension benefits when they retire.

47 Selected Supreme Court Decisions - Eeoc ... - Eeoc Home Page, https://www.eeoc.gov/eeoc/history/35th/thelaw/supreme_court.html (accessed November 8, 2017).

48 Milestones: 1977 - Equal Employment Opportunity Commission, https://www.eeoc.gov/eeoc/history/50th/milestones/1977.cfm?renderforprint=1 (accessed November 8, 2017).

Payroll, Taxes, Compliance, Oh My!

Compliance and the IRS

Staying compliant with the States and IRS is one of your highest priorities, so you don't want to make errors or receive fines from the IRS.

Five steps you need to take to stay compliant.

There are five key steps to take to stay compliant with your State and the IRS:

1. Make sure that all your calculations are perfect. The number one thing businesses get penalized for is simple arithmetic mistakes.

2. Make all of your deposits on a timely basis. Every. Single. One.

3. Know every return you need to file for all entities that tax you in your State and locality.

4. File all your returns on a timely basis. Even if you have to file a return that is wrong. File it on time and amend it later. Then you won't be penalized for late filing.

5. Answer all correspondences you receive. Taxing entities lose things and misplace them constantly.

6. Bonus: Keep detailed records of what, when, how, and make copies.

There are numerous **federal employment tax penalties on the payroll side of the business**. They include:

- Failure to deposit taxes (withholding and Federal Unemployment).

- Failure to deposit taxes timely (you have to know your deposit period).

- Failure to deposit enough tax money.

- Failure to file a tax return (at a minimum Form 941 and Form 940).

- Failure to file a tax return timely.

- Failure to file a complete tax return.

- Failure to file W2s.

- Failure to file 1099s.

- Failure to file W2s timely.

- Failure to file 1099s timely.

- Failure to file W2s that tie with the quarterly 941s you filed.

Then you have practically the same thing for the State Revenue and State Unemployment departments. These can be very serious problems. **Some of the fines can be 100% of the tax due.** Sometimes there are penalties for late or missing returns even if there is no tax due.

In addition to employment tax penalties, there are a number of **employment-related laws that many business owners break unknowingly.** Some of them include:

1. Misclassification of workers as Independent Contractors instead of employees.

2. Misclassification of exempt versus nonexempt employees.

3. Inappropriate questions in the hiring process.

4. Paying in cash under the table.

5. Abuse of training wages.

6. Paying Comp time instead of overtime.

7. Not paying overtime properly.

8. Not paying minimum wage amount when paying by piece work.

9. Not reporting 1099 payments above $600.00.

10. Hiring undocumented workers.

11. Not maintaining personnel files with I-9s and documents or W-4.

12. Gender pay inequality.

13. Misclassification certain benefits as pre-tax versus post tax.

14. Docking exempt employees incorrectly for missing hours.

15. Not understanding Child Labor laws.

16. Not understanding pre-tax restrictions.

17. Not withholding Child Support payments.

18. Not doing new hire reporting.

19. Payroll debit cards that don't meet State regulations.

20. Not having Section 125 Cafeteria Plan on file.

21. Discriminatory retirement plans.

22. Not getting signatures on non-statutory deductions.

23. Illegal deductions from employees checks.

24. Not providing pay stubs that meet state law.

25. Not securing payroll information from identity theft hacks.

26. Not truncating Social Security numbers of documents.

27. Paying W-2 compensation to the owner, if not incorporated.

28. The list goes on...

Seven things to do when the IRS penalizes you.

1. The first thing to remember is that IRS cannot penalize you for a simple mistake. It has to be gross negligence. There is no fixed definition of gross negligence in the tax code. It is at the discretion of the IRS or finally the courts.

2. If your mistake results in paying fewer taxes, pay the tax immediately. That stops additional interest and penalties on the actual tax amount.

3. Write the IRS at the address on the letter. Explain what happened. There are some things the IRS may accept. Ask for an abatement (reversal) of the penalty and the interest. They will probably not abate the interest on the tax amount but may well abate the penalty. If they refuse to abate the penalty, they will give you an appeal route. Send the next letter. Make sure your letters lay out the rationale for the abatement in detail. You may not get a chance to add to the circumstances or reasoning later.

4. Keep all correspondences. Keep notes on any phone calls. Always get the IRS employee's ID number and the name and if possible a call back number or at least an address.

5. If the second letter does not work, write a third. Send this letter to the Appeals Division where the most knowledgeable people work. You have an excellent chance of getting an abatement here.

6. Remember these are people with an impossible job. They deal with irate people all day long many times enforcing laws that Congress passed that make little or no economic sense, and they know it. Be nice to them. Be friendly. Laugh! They tend to return the attitude they get from taxpayers. You will get the occasional bad attitude, many times you can excuse yourself and call back, getting a different person with a better attitude.

7. If offered a Collection Due Process (CDP) hearing take it. This may be the best shot at getting a resolution. It also stops all collection activity in most cases. The IRS employees holding the hearings have a good deal of latitude and a lot of knowledge. Restate in detail or even attach copies of your previous letters to the request.

8. Bonus Tip: If all else fails, see if you can file a Pro Se (on one's own behalf) Petition with the US Tax Court. The vast majority of cases (over 95%) are settled before they ever go to court. It also stops the collection process until the case is closed.

IRS Letters. What are they and what do they mean?

There are many different types of letters that you could receive from the IRS that range among these topics

- Levy
- Balance Due
- Information Request
- Installment Agreement
- Address Update
- Taxpayer Info Request
- Locate Taxpayer
- Employment Tax

- Filing
- Refund
- Zero Balance
- Federal Tax Deposit
- Penalty
- Credits
- Combined Annual Wage Reconciliation
- and more.

We've included a list of them below. For more information about each form, search the Notice Number on the IRS website. Some of these notices you will want to act on, and we've noted those as well.

Notice Number (View details on IRS.gov)	Description	Topic
LT11	We haven't received any payment from you for your overdue taxes. This letter is to advise you of our intent to seize your property or rights to property. You must contact us immediately. *The LT11 is a critical letter. If you get a letter, your next step is to file a petition in US Tax Court. The alternative is to pay the taxes requested and file for a refund. When it is denied file in US District Court.* *DO NOT IGNORE THIS LETTER!*	Levy
LT14	We show you have past due taxes and we've been unable to reach you. Call us immediately.	Balance Due
LT16 A/B/C/D/E/F/G	We may take enforcement action to collect taxes you owe because you have not responded to previous notices we sent you on this matter. We need to hear from you about your overdue taxes or tax returns.	Balance Due
LT18	We have not received a response from you to our previous requests for overdue tax returns.	Balance Due
LT24	We received your payment proposal to pay the tax you owe; however, we need more information about your financial situation.	Balance Due
LT26	You were previously asked information regarding the filing of your tax return for a specific tax period.	Information Request
LT27	For us to consider an installment agreement for your overdue taxes, you must complete Form 433F, Collection Information Statement.	Installment Agreement

LT33	We received your payment; however, there's still an outstanding balance.	Balance Due
LT39	We're required by law to remind you in writing about your overdue tax.	Balance Due
LT40	We're trying to collect unpaid taxes from you. To do so, we may contact others to get or verify your contact information. *This one means they are going to contact family, friends, vendors, employee and other trying to find you.*	Balance Due
LT41	We're trying to collect unfiled returns from you. To do so, we may contact others to get or verify your contact information. *This one means they are going to contact family, friends, vendors, employee and other trying to find you.*	Balance Due
LP47	We are requesting your assistance in locating a taxpayer that may or may not be currently employed by you.	Address Update
LP59	We previously sent you a notice of levy to collect money from the taxpayer named in the notice but received no response or an explanation of why you haven't sent it.	Levy
LP60	We need information about a possible deceased taxpayer to help resolve a federal tax matter.	Information request
LP61	We need information about a taxpayer to assist us in resolving a federal tax matter.	Taxpayer Info Request
LP62	We need information about a taxpayer to assist us in resolving a federal tax matter. We are asking for your help because we believe this person has an account with you.	Taxpayer Info Request

LP64	We are requesting your assistance in trying to locate a taxpayer that you may or may not know.	Locate Taxpayer
LP68	We released the notice of levy sent to you regarding the taxpayer named in the notice.	Levy
LT73	Your federal employment tax is still not paid. We issued a notice levy to collect your unpaid taxes.	Employment Tax
LT75	Your federal tax is unpaid. We asked you to pay the tax but haven't received your payment. We issued a notice of levy to collect your unpaid taxes.	Levy
CP080	We credited payments and other credits to your tax account for the form and tax period shown on your notice. However, we haven't received your tax return.	Filing
CP081	We haven't received your tax return for a specific tax year. The statute of limitations to claim a refund of your credit or payment for that tax year is about to expire.	Filing
CP101	We made changes to your return because we believe there's a miscalculation. You owe money on your taxes as a result of these changes.	Balance Due
CP102	We made changes to your return because we believe there's a miscalculation. You owe money on your taxes as a result of these changes.	Balance Due
CP103	We made changes to your tax return because we found a miscalculation. As a result of these changes, your balance due also changed.	Balance Due
CP104	We made changes to your excise tax return because we believe there was a miscalculation. As a result of these changes, there is a balance due.	Balance Due

CP105	We made changes to your tax return because we found a miscalculation. As a result of these changes, you have a balance due.	Balance Due
CP106	We believe you have miscalculations on your return. The changes we made resulted in a balance due.	Balance Due
CP107	We made changes to your Form 1042, Annual Withholding Tax Return for U.S. Source Income of Foreign Persons because we found a miscalculation. As a result of these changes, you have a balance due.	Balance Due
CP108	You are receiving this notice because you made a payment of $XXXXX on XXXXX, and we can't determine the correct form or tax year to apply it to.	Payment
CP111	We made changes to your return because we believe there's a miscalculation. As a result, you are due to a refund.	Refund
CP112	We made changes to your return because we believe there's a miscalculation. As a result, you are due to a refund.	Refund
CP114	We made changes to your excise tax return because we believe there was a miscalculation. As a result of these changes, there is an overpayment on your account.	Refund
CP115	We made changes to your tax return because we found a miscalculation. As a result of these changes, you have an overpayment on your account.	Refund
CP116	We believe you have miscalculations on your return. The changes we made resulted in a refund.	Refund

CP125	We made changes to your tax return because we found a miscalculation. As a result of these changes, you have a balance due of less than $1.	Balance Due
CP126	We believe you have miscalculations on your return, and we changed it.	Balance Due
CP128	You received this notice because of the remaining balance due on a tax period after an overpayment was applied to your account.	Balance Due
CP131	We made changes to your tax return because we believe there's a miscalculation on your return. As a result of these changes, you don't owe us any money, nor are you due to a refund.	Zero Balance
CP131A	We made changes to your tax return because we believe there's a miscalculation on your return. As a result of these changes, you don't owe us any money, nor are you due to a refund.	Zero Balance
CP132	We made changes to your tax return because we believe there's a miscalculation on your return. As a result of these changes, you owe an additional amount.	Balance Due
CP133	We made changes to your tax return because we believe there's a miscalculation on your return. As a result of these changes, there's an overpayment on your account.	Refund
CP134B	This balance due notice alerts you there is a discrepancy in some federal tax deposits credited to your account from the amount reported on your tax return, and to make payment by the pay-by-date listed on the notice.	FTD Federal Tax Deposit

CP134R	This notice tells you a discrepancy exists between the amounts of federal tax deposits credited to your account from the amount reported on your tax return. Therefore, you're due to a refund.	FTD Federal Tax Deposit
CP136	The CP136 explains your deposit requirements for your Form 941 filings for next year, which may be different from your requirements for last year. We base your deposit requirement on the total tax you reported on your Forms 941 for the four previous consecutive quarterly periods (the lookback period).	FTD Federal Tax Deposit
CP136B	The CP136B explains your deposit requirements for your Form 941filings for next year, which may be different from your requirements for last year. We base your deposit requirement on the total tax you reported on your Form 944 last year.	FTD Federal Tax Deposit
CP137	Your deposit requirements for Form 943 for next year may be different, based on your Form 943 tax from last year.	FTD Federal Tax Deposit
CP138	This notice tells you that all or part of the overpayment on a return you filed was applied to other federal taxes you owe.	Offset
CP141C	You are receiving this notice because you did not respond to a previous request for missing or incomplete information on your return and your return is late.	Filing
CP141I	You are receiving this notice because you did not respond to a previous request for missing or incomplete information on your return.	Filing

CP141L	You are receiving this notice because you didn't file your return by the due date.	Filing
CP141R	We removed the penalty charged on your account.	Penalty
CP142	We sent you this notice because you filed your information returns late.	Filing
CP143	We accepted your explanation for filing your information return late. We will continue processing your returns.	Filing
CP145	We were unable to credit the full amount you requested to the succeeding tax period.	Credits
CP152	We have received your return.	Confirmation of Return Receipt
CP153	We can't provide you with your refund through direct deposit, so we're sending you a refund check/credit payment by mail.	Refund
CP160	You received this notice to remind you of the amount you owe in tax, penalty, and interest.	Balance Due
CP161	You received this notice because you have an unpaid balance due.	Balance Due
CP163	You received this notice to remind you of the amount you owe in tax, penalty, and interest.	Balance Due
CP165	We sent you this notice because your bank didn't honor your payment. As a result, we charged you a penalty.	Payment
CP166	We were unable to process your monthly payment because there were insufficient funds in your bank account.	Payment
CP169	You received this notice because we couldn't locate the return you said was previously filed.	Filing

CP171	You received this notice to remind you of the amount you owe in tax, penalty, and interest.	Balance Due
CP177	We are notifying you of our intent to levy certain assets for unpaid taxes. You have the right to a Collection Due Process hearing. *If you receive this letter, you will very probably want to take advantage of a Collection Due Process Hearing. There will be a time limit for filing the Form 12153. Don't miss it.*	Levy
CP180/CP181	We sent you this notice because your tax return is missing a schedule or form.	Filing
CP187	You received this notice to remind you of the amount you owe in tax, penalty, and interest.	Balance Due
CP188	We are holding your refund until we determine you owe no other taxes.	Refund
CP207	You received this notice because of your deposit schedule, the Record of Federal Tax Liability (ROFTL), had missing or incorrect information. We need additional information from you.	FTD Federal Tax Deposit
CP207L	You received this notice because of your deposit schedule, the Record of Federal Tax Liability (ROFTL), had missing or incorrect information. We need additional information from you.	FTD Federal Tax Deposit
CP210/CP220	We made a change(s) for the tax year specified in the notice.	Payment
CP225	We applied a payment to your account.	Payment

CP230	The amounts shown on your information returns differed from the amounts shown on your employment tax returns. As a result of this discrepancy, you owe an additional amount.	CAWR Combined Annual Wage Reconciliation
CP231	Your refund or credit payment was returned to us, and we need you to update your current address.	Address Update Needed
CP235	The CP235 is issued when it appears that you are using the prior year's deposit schedule when you are required to use a different deposit schedule.	Taxpayer Inquiry
CP236	Your deposit requirements were changed from monthly to semi-weekly. CP236 is a reminder that you may not be following the semi-weekly deposit schedule timeframe correctly. *Missing this notice is the cause of many penalties. It is telling you that you should be depositing your employment taxes on a semi-weekly basis instead of the monthly basis you were filing. Failure to change results in late deposits, penalties, and interest.*	Taxpayer Inquiry
CP238	The CP238 tells you we can waive federal tax deposit penalties for the first time you file a specific tax form.	Taxpayer Inquiry
CP240	There's a discrepancy between the information you reported on your employment tax return and figures submitted to us from your W-2, W-2G, and 1099R forms. As a result of this discrepancy, you owe an additional amount.	CAWR Combined Annual Wage Reconciliation

CP248	We issued this notice when you didn't make a Federal Tax Deposit (FTD) through an approved electronic method such as the Electronic Federal Tax Payment System (EFTPS).	EFTPS Electronic Federal Tax Payment System
CP250A	This notice informs you that your annual federal employment tax filing requirement has changed.	Filing requirement
CP250B	This notice informs you that your annual federal employment tax filing requirement has not changed for the current calendar year.	Filing requirement
CP250C	This notice informs you that your annual federal employment tax filing requirement has changed.	Filing requirement
CP254	Your organization submitted a paper return for the tax period in question. Because our records show that you must file electronically, the paper return does not satisfy your filing obligation.	E-file
CP259	We show that you are required to file a tax return for the tax periods indicated on your notice but haven't.	Filing
CP260	We removed a payment that was incorrectly applied to your tax return for the tax period shown on your notice. This notice shows the correct amount you owe us.	Payment
CP261	CP261 is the approval notice for Form 2553, Election by a Small Business Corporation.	Filing
CP262	CP 262 generates when IRS revokes a Subchapter S election.	S-Corporation
CP264	CP264 is the notice for denial of Form 2553, Election by a Small Business Corporation.	Filing

CP265	CP 265 generates when IRS terminates a Subchapter S election.	S-Corporation
CP266	This notice generates when Chief Counsel receives a referral of your Form 2553, Election by a Small Business Corporation.	S-Corporation
CP267	The amount of credits (federal tax deposits or estimated tax payments) you claimed on your tax return for the tax period shown on your notice and some credits that were applied to that year are different.	FTD
CP268	We made changes to your return because we believe there is a miscalculation on your return. You have a potential overpayment credit because of this miscalculation.	Credits
CP276A	We didn't receive a correctly completed tax liability schedule. We normally charge a Federal Tax Deposit (FTD) penalty when this happens. We decided not to do so this time.	FTD Penalty
CP276B	We didn't receive the correct amount of tax deposits. We normally charge a Federal Tax Deposit penalty when this happens. We decided not to do so this time.	FTD Penalty
CP297	We are notifying you of our intent to levy certain assets for unpaid taxes. You have the right to a Collection Due Process hearing.	Levy
CP297A	We levied your assets for unpaid taxes. You have the right to a Collection Due Process hearing.	Levy
CP297C	We levied your assets for unpaid taxes. You have the right to a Collection Due Process hearing.	Levy

CP298	We are notifying you of our intent to levy up to 15% of your social security benefits for unpaid taxes.	Levy
CP504	You have an unpaid amount due on your account. If you do not pay the amount due immediately, the IRS will seize (levy) your state income tax refund and apply it to pay the amount you owe.	Levy
CP504B	You have an unpaid amount due on your account. If you do not pay the amount due immediately, the IRS will seize (levy) certain property or rights to property and apply it to pay the amount you owe. *These two are quite common in light of a deposit problem on either the taxpayer's part or by the IRS. **It is important to answer, but it is not the last notice before they levy. That is normally the LT11.***	Levy
CP515B	This reminder notice tells you our records show you did not file a business tax return.	Filing
CP518B	This is a final reminder notice that we still have no record that you filed your prior tax returns.	Filing
CP2000	The income and payment information we have on file doesn't match the information you reported on your tax return. This could affect your tax return; it may cause an increase or decrease in your tax, or may not change it at all.	Under Reporter
CP2005	We accepted the information you sent us. We're not going to change your tax return. We've closed our review of it.	Under Reporter
CP2006	We received your information. We'll look at it and let you know what we're going to do.	Under Reporter

CP2057	You need to file an amended return. We've received information not reported on your tax return.	Under Reporter
CP2501	You need to contact us. We've received information not reported on your tax return.	Under Reporter
LT2531	Information reported on your tax return doesn't match the information reported to us.	Under Reporter
Letter 0484C	Collection Information Statement Requested (Form 433F/433D); Inability to Pay/Transfer	Request for Information
Letter 0549C	Balance Due on Account is Paid	Balance Due
Letter 0681C	Proposal to Pay Accepted	Payment

Relevant forms to help you stay compliant.

We've included a list and a link to forms that we think are relevant in keeping your business compliant with the IRS and the States.

IRS

Employer's QUARTERLY Federal Tax Return Form 941
https://www.irs.gov/pub/irs-pdf/f941.pdf

Adjusted Employer's QUARTERLY Federal Tax Return or Claim for Refund Form 941X
https://www.irs.gov/pub/irs-pdf/f941x.pdf

Employer's Annual Federal Unemployment (FUTA) Tax Return Form 940
https://www.irs.gov/pub/irs-pdf/f940.pdf

Wage and Tax Statement Form W-2
https://www.irs.gov/pub/irs-pdf/fw2.pdf

Corrected Wage and Tax Statement Form W-2C
https://www.irs.gov/pub/irs-pdf/fw2c.pdf

Transmittal of Wage and Tax Statements Form W-3
https://www.irs.gov/pub/irs-pdf/fw3.pdf

Transmittal of Corrected Wage and Tax Statements Form W-3C
https://www.irs.gov/pub/irs-pdf/fw3c.pdf

Miscellaneous Income Form 1099 Misc
https://www.irs.gov/pub/irs-pdf/f1099msc.pdf

Annual Summary and Transmittal of U.S. Information Returns Form 1096
https://www.irs.gov/pub/irs-pdf/f1096.pdf

States

Get your State Tax Withholding Forms on the Bureau of Labor Statistics website here: https://www.bls.gov/jobs/statetax.htm

Don't forget your local tax, if applicable.

Some states require local taxes. For example, "Employers with worksites located in Pennsylvania are required to withhold and remit the local Earned Income Tax (EIT) and Local Services Tax (LST) on behalf of their employees working in PA. Examples of business worksites include, but are not limited to: factories, warehouses, branches, offices and residences of home-based employees." (source: http://dced.pa.gov/local-government/local-income-tax-information/)

Here is a link to the Pennsylvania local taxing authority and a list of forms for the employer:

- https://www.hab-inc.com/forms/
- https://www.hab-inc.com/forms/forms-for-employers/

Create a tax calendar.

It's extremely important never to miss a filing date. Mark your calendars every year with these dates with reminder alerts, so you file on-time. This simple step could save you.

The following are some of the more significant filing dates for a corporation using a calendar year-end. Many of these requirements also apply to partnerships and sole proprietorships. Naturally, if a year-end other than December 31st is used some of these dates will vary. Most small businesses, however, use December 31st as their year-end.

JANUARY 15TH

File and pay fourth estimated tax payment.

JANUARY 31ST

Send out IRS Form W-2 for the previous year.

Pay any undeposited federal unemployment tax and file IRS Form 940.

On IRS Form 941, report wages and tax related to employees' wages of the previous quarter (income, FICA, Medicare) - pay any undeposited withheld tax.

Pay previous quarter's state unemployment tax and file a quarterly report with the state revenue agency.

Form W-3, report wage information to the Social Security Administration - include copies of all W-2s - make no payment.

MARCH 15TH

Pay and file corporate income tax (Form 1120 or Form 1120S).

File for six-month corporate tax extension with Form 7004 — pay estimated tax.

Deadline to file Form 2553 for S corporation election for this calendar year.

APRIL 15TH

Pay and file personal income tax Form 1040.

File automatic six-month extension and pay estimated taxes (1040).

File first estimated tax payment.

APRIL 30TH

On IRS Form 941, report wages and tax related to employees' wages of the previous quarter (income, FICA, Medicare) - pay any undeposited withheld tax.

Deposit federal unemployment tax for a previous quarter if more than $100.

Pay the previous quarter's state unemployment tax and file "Employer's Quarterly Report."

JUNE 15TH

File second estimated tax payment.

JULY 31ST

On IRS Form 941, report wages and tax related to employees' wages of the previous quarter (income, FICA, Medicare) - pay any undeposited withheld tax.

Deposit federal unemployment tax for a previous quarter if more than $100.

Pay previous quarter's state unemployment tax and quarterly file report with the state revenue agency.

SEPTEMBER 15TH

Pay and file corporate income tax (1120/1102S) - previously extended.

Pay third estimated tax payment.

OCTOBER 15TH

Pay and file personal income tax (1040/1041) - those extended twice.

OCTOBER 31ST

On IRS Form 941, report wages and tax related to employees' wages of the previous quarter (income, FICA, Medicare) - pay any undeposited withheld tax.

Deposit federal unemployment tax for a previous quarter if more than $100.

Pay previous quarter's state unemployment tax and quarterly file report with the state revenue agency.

Chapter 1

What about tax deposit penalties? What are they?

Penalties may apply if you

1. do not make required deposits on time,

2. make deposits for less than the required amount, or

3. do not use EFTPS when required.

The penalties do not apply if any failure to make a proper and timely deposit was due to reasonable cause and not to willful neglect.

For amounts not properly or timely deposited, the penalty rates on tax deposits made 6 to 15 days late:

2%	Tax Deposits made 1 to 5 days late.
5%	Tax Deposits made 6 to 15 days late.
10%	Tax Deposits made 16 or more days late. Also, applies to amounts paid within ten days of the date of the first notice the IRS sent asking for the tax due.
10%	Tax Deposits made at an unauthorized financial institution paid directly to the IRS or paid with your tax return.
10%	Tax Deposit amounts subject to electronic deposit requirements but not deposited using EFTPS.
15%	Tax Deposit amounts still unpaid more than ten days after the date of the first notice that the IRS sent asking for the tax due or the day on which you received notice and demand for immediate payment, whichever is earlier.

Late tax deposit penalty amounts are determined using calendar days, starting from the due date of the liability.

Order in which tax deposits are applied.

Tax deposits are applied to the most recent tax liability within the quarter. If you receive a failure-to-deposit penalty notice, you may designate how your payment is to be applied to minimize the amount of the penalty. Follow the instructions on the penalty notice that you received.

For more information on designating deposits, see Rev. Proc. 2001-58. You can find Rev. Proc. 2001-58 on page 579 of Internal Revenue Bulletin 2001-50 at http://www.IRS.gov/pub/IRS-irbs/irb01-50.pdf

Example: Cedar, Inc. is required to deposit $1,000 on June 15 and $1,500 on July 15. It does not deposit on June 15. On July 15, Cedar, Inc. deposits $2,000. Under the deposits rule, which applies deposits to the most recent tax liability, $1,500 of the deposit is applied to the July 15 deposit and the remaining $500 is applied to the June deposit. Accordingly, $500 of the June 15 liability remains undeposited. The penalty on this under deposit will apply as explained above.

Trust fund recovery penalty.

If income, Social Security, and Medicare taxes that must be withheld are not withheld or are not deposited or paid to the United States Treasury, the trust fund recovery penalty may apply. The penalty is the full amount of the unpaid trust fund tax. This penalty may apply to you if these unpaid taxes cannot be immediately collected from the employer or business.

The trust fund recovery penalty may be imposed on all persons who are determined by the IRS to be responsible for collecting, accounting for, and paying over these taxes, and who acted willfully in not doing so. A responsible person can be an officer or Employee of a corporation, a partner or Employee of a partnership, an accountant, a volunteer director/trustee, or an Employee of a sole proprietorship. A responsible person also may include one who signs checks for the business or otherwise has authority to cause the spending of business funds.

Willfully means voluntarily, consciously, and intentionally. A responsible person acts willfully if the person knows that the required actions are not taking place.[1]

Separate accounting may be required when deposits are not made or withheld taxes are not paid.

Separate accounting may be required if you do not pay over withheld Employee Social Security, Medicare, or income taxes; deposit required taxes; make required payments; or file tax returns. In this case, you would receive written notice from the IRS requiring you to deposit taxes into a special trust account for the U.S. Government. You would also have to file monthly tax returns on Form 941-M, Employer's Monthly Federal Tax Return.

While it may seem daunting to stay compliant with the IRS, and even a little bit scary if you receive a letter from them, it's important to keep a level head, read what the notification is about, and take one step at a time to resolve it.

1 Depositing Federal Income, Social Security & Medicare Taxes, http://www.rlsire.com/FAQ/FrequentlyAskedQuestions_files/content/Fed_deposit.htm (accessed November 9, 2017).

How to beat the IRS at its own game.

What to do when you get a letter from the IRS.

"Payroll taxes are due, with penalties and interest"

At least that is what the letter from the IRS says. First thing, don't panic. Quoting Daniel J. Pilla's study for the Cato Institute *"About 40 percent of the revenues the IRS collects through penalty assessments are abated when citizens challenge the penalties."* So we now know the odds are good that the IRS is wrong or will blink first.[1]

What do we do?

Before we dive into that, let's review what some "normal" problems with payroll taxes include.

- A failure to File a return.
- Taxes are under-reported.
- Taxes are under-deposited.
- Taxes are deposited late.
- IRS mistakes.

1 Payroll Tax Penalties, When The Irs Sends A Letter. - Www .., https://www.ralphcoutard.com/payroll-tax-penalties-when-the-irs-sends-a-letter/ (accessed November 9, 2017).

Any of these can create a situation where the IRS charges penalties and interest against a business and then adds up subsequent tax deposits creating additional late and short payments simply exacerbating the situation. We will get to that later.

What does the letter from the IRS mean?

Each letter will normally tell you the issue that resulted in the letter, but, not always. The jargon can get convoluted, and it is written in IRS speak. It's not something we normally speak in conversation, only behind closed doors. But it still requires an answer. *Do not make the mistake of not answering a letter.* It may make no difference if you don't answer. But it might. Always answer, in writing, every letter, and keep copies of their letter and your reply.

If you don't understand what the letter says, write and ask for clarification. **The IRS assumes, often incorrectly, that you received, read and understood previous communications.**

If for any reason, you didn't get or remember the previous letter you will be starting off in the middle of the movie. I don't suggest calling the IRS at the number they list on the letter. You are better off writing and asking for information so you have it in writing, rather than notes from a telephone call.

Many times you can look up terms, forms, publications, code sections and regulations right on the IRS website www.irs.gov. Sometimes those will be confusing as well. If there is a phrase or term you still don't understand, Google it. There will usually be numerous entries of people trying to explain what is going on and sell you on allowing them to handle it for a fee. You are most likely not the only one who doesn't understand something in an IRS letter, however, take your Google results with a grain of salt.

How do you answer the Internal Revenue Service?

When you answer the IRS, there are several important things to remember.

- Don't give them more information than which they ask. Never volunteer anything unless you are absolutely sure it is to your advantage.

- Always answer back the person or office that wrote you to start. You may want to send copies to other offices or agents if there is some reason to do so. For example, if the letter comes from Ogden don't send your reply to Austin even if that is where you filed the original return. Sometimes you will have more than one office of the IRS writing to you about the same tax and tax period. In that case, send a copy of your letter to the first office, second office and mark it as a copy. Do not be scared to inundate the IRS with paper.

- Include identifying information that was included in the letter you received. You can also include a copy of the letter you received if you have any doubt about making yourself clear. I have been known to highlight a copy of the IRS letter and send it back to them with my cover letter.

One of the things to keep in mind is to thread your narrative needs to remain constant. Before you answer the very first letter about a situation, know exactly what your story is and remain consistent. If you don't know how the story should be relayed, ask your CPA. If he understands employment tax problems, he may be able to help you. If he is not conversant and you have doubts about what you should say find a CPA who handles employment tax problems on a regular basis, it is a specialty. If all else fails, you can call me.

You can start out with less detail and add more detail as you go, but I have found it is better to have as much detail as possible from the start. Anything that helps show that this is not gross negligence is always desirable. The more detail of people, place, time, location and what was going on makes the presentation even more believable. You are telling a story. Hopefully, it is true, but a story nonetheless. You need to flesh it out and make it tell the story you want in the most believable way possible.

Let's jump back into what is considered "Normal" payroll tax problems.

A failure to file a return. "The IRS says you never filed a return. They may create a return for you. They will estimate taxes due in an amount they know exceeds what would be reasonably due based on your account. They do this to get your attention. Many people, if the estimated amount were too low, would just pay it. The IRS does not want that to happen, so they always overestimate if they create a "Substitute Return" and file it for you.[2]

2 Payroll Tax Penalties, When The Irs Sends A Letter – Smart .., https://www.smartservicesla.org/blog/payroll-tax-penalties-when-the-irs-sends-a- (accessed November 9, 2017).

What to do: The answer to that is to send a copy of the return. If you filed it certified mail, send a copy of the receipt when it was sent proving the date and a copy of the return receipt showing it was received.

> **A tip** *is never to mail more than one return in an envelope. The clerk opening the envelope may staple them together, and only the top return will ever get reported as being received.*

If you didn't send it certified in your accompanying letter talk about your history of filing on time and this one was surely just misrouted. If you have collateral proof of the filing date of a canceled check that was sent with the returned quote that information or even includes copies. If the return was due on the 15th and the check attached cleared your bank on the 18th that is pretty convincing that the report was there by the 15th.

Taxes are under-reported. Find out why they say that. Did the IRS transpose a number when they manually entered the return? That happens with regularity. Have they just pulled a number out of their hat? That happens periodically. Once we received two notices from two different customers on the same day saying they had overpaid their 940 taxes and offering them each a refund of over $36,000.00 each. The total 940 tax deposits for the two clients combined were less than $2000.00. And no, I did not let them apply for and receive the checks.)[3]

What to do: Send the IRS a copy of the return that you filed. If the return is wrong, send the IRS a corrected form such as a **941-X** to correct the original filing. For instance, if you put second-quarter figures on the third quarter report. There wouldn't be a penalty for late filing if, in fact, you filed an original return on time even if it was incorrect.

> **A tip:** *If you cannot prepare the actual return on time, estimate it and file it. Then file a corrected return when you can, this avoids a late filing fee.*[4]

Taxes are under-deposited. The IRS says you made fewer or smaller deposits than you reported. Check their list and dates of deposits against yours. Don't accept their word for it. You should have the proof in your files.

> **Be aware**: *We have noticed a real problem recently. EFTPS payments are not being shown with the date in the electronic file the same as on the "IRS Statement of Account."*

Have they applied the payment to the wrong period? We see it constantly that regardless of what we tell EFTPS in the electronic submission of the payments that

3 Ibid.

4 Payroll Tax Penalties, When The Irs Sends A Letter – Smart .., https://www.smartservicesla.org/blog/payroll-tax-penalties-when-the-irs-sends-a- (accessed November 9, 2017).

the IRS moves it forward a period. Also, if they think there is an old amount due they will apply a current payment to the old amount due creating additional penalties. If you tell the IRS where to apply for the payment as you do through EFTPS, they are required to post it there. Don't let them tell you otherwise.

What to do: Prepare the data showing your proof that you made the payments on time, bank statements, EFTPS confirmations or whatever proof you have. Make copies and mail them to the IRS with a letter of explanation, and a request for them to update their records.

If in fact, you missed a deposit, it happens, make it immediately and ask for abatement anyway. If you inadvertently missed the deposit, cite valid reasons for the occurrence. Discuss steps you have taken to make sure it won't happen again. They cannot penalize you for a simple mistake, only gross negligence.

Taxes are deposited late. If you deposit your taxes late, you can follow the same steps as the previous section - taxes under deposited - to try and fix it.

What to do: Document everything and mail letters to the IRS. Don't give up! If the first person at the IRS turns you down that doesn't mean the next one will.

> **A tip**: *The IRS will usually reject the initial request for a penalty abatement. Communicating with IRS representatives usually result in a series of no's before you get your yes. Once you get it, walk away.*

> **Be aware**: One of the favorite tricks of the IRS involves a string of deposits.

> "Let's say you were supposed to make 12 deposits of $1000.00 each the 15th of each month starting February 15th and ending January 15th for January through December. The second deposit is missing, and the check never got cashed. You don't know what happened.[5] The IRS will take the third payment and apply it to the second month's taxes, but it is late, so they charge a penalty. Now the fourth month's deposit gets applied to the third month's taxes, but it is also a month late, so there is another late paying penalty. You will quickly have ten late payment penalties and the 12th month penalized as not being paid at all. The penalties exceed the taxes missing."

The IRS cannot do this though they will try. If you designate the third deposit for the third-month taxes, they must apply for payment there, period. **If they don't record the deposit the way you designated, you can force them to do so**. It is their regulations that says they must follow it. Do not accept all the penalties, only the one month. Then, ask for an abatement. The IRS is supposed to give you a pass on the first penalty.

5 Payroll Tax Penalties, When The Irs Sends A Letter – Smart .., https://www.smartservicesla.org/blog/payroll-tax-penalties-when-the-irs-sends-a- (accessed November 9, 2017).

The further caveat on this is that if there is an overpayment/refund. The IRS will automatically apply it to the oldest outstanding debt. There is very little you can do about that if it happens.

IRS mistakes.

How do you show the IRS that you are right and they are wrong?
The IRS makes untold egregious errors every day!

- They post things to the wrong place.

- They post money to the wrong account.

- They lose or misplace reports.

- They staple two reports together, and the bottom one is effectively lost forever.

- They misinterpret the law and regulations.

- They ignore the law and their regulations.

- They don't know the law and their regulations.

The tax law is so complex no one knows it all. **No One**.

Many of these agents and officers are new and poorly trained. The best agents get promoted and are not on the front lines anymore. They are pressured to produce revenue even if none is due. Revenue agents don't get promoted for zero change or audits that result in refunds.

If the IRS makes a mistake what do you do?

Don't get mad. That serves no good purpose and will only hurt you. If you take the typical attitude that the IRS messed up, and you're going to yell and scream at them, even in writing, they will just ignore you, and the problem goes away for them. Yes, the IRS actually does that. It goes to collection and collection does not care if you owe the money or not.

Collection representatives assume compliance handles that and that if you transferred to the collections division you owe the money, and it is not their job to see if it is right or wrong. They are paid only to collect. So don't upset the compliance officers unnecessarily, they will just let the case go to collections and say adios.

Write a letter to the IRS.

1. Write your letter with calm and deliberation.

2. Write it clearly and dispassionately.

3. Point out the facts logically and straightforwardly. Be like Joe Friday in Dragnet, "The facts Ma'am, just the facts."

4. Point out the error. Tell the IRS agent in detail why what the IRS says is in error.

5. Back it up with documents and other proof.

What if you did make an error?

"The penalties do not apply if any failure to make a proper and timely deposit was due to reasonable cause and not to willful neglect. (IRC 6656 and others)".[6] (Source: **IRS: The IRS Publication 15 Circular E)**

If you have a valid business reason that a penalty has occurred in spite of good due diligence on your part the IRS is supposed to abate the penalty.[7]

Understand that IRS employees may be gauged by how much revenue they bring in (the IRS vehemently denies this, but ex IRS employees have said otherwise). When that is true, they don't want to abate penalties regardless.

One trick they have is to offer a reduced penalty as a favor, when in fact they should have zeroed it out. Another is the IRS "will offer to abate penalties on two quarters if you pay the third. It is normally not a good idea to accept these offers.

---

6   Publication 15 - Circular E, Employer's Tax Guide - 11 .., https://taxmap.irs.gov/taxmap/archive2012/taxmap/pubs/p15-010.htm (accessed November 10, 2017).

7   Payroll Tax Penalties, When The Irs Sends A Letter – Smart .., https://www.smartservicesla.org/blog/payroll-tax-penalties-when-the-irs-sends-a- (accessed November 10, 2017).

You can do better. Keep writing letters and filing documents at the higher and higher levels until one person gets reasonable and says yes. Then take that yes and run. [8]

Can an ordinary citizen do this? Sure! Is it easier for a payroll tax professional? Sure! The IRS is far more likely to listen to a CPA than a citizen. The CPA knows what buttons to push and how to go to the next level. An ordinary citizen may not. The CPA is far less likely to get emotionally involved than the citizen with the emptying pocket.

Your payroll service provider should have CPAs on staff to handle these situations for you. If not, seriously consider a payroll service provider that does. Because when not if, the IRS makes an error your regular CPA will charge you full rate to solve problems that should be solved by your payroll provider for free." [9]

If you want a heavyweight on your side, ask your payroll provider if they have a USTCP (The United States Tax Court Practitioner) on staff that can assist you. A USTCP is a professional usually an EA or CPA who is specially licensed to represent clients in tax court while not being an attorney.

Appeals

After writing your first and second letter and the IRS has denied any abatement, the third letter should normally get directed to the Appeals Division of the IRS. It's not a bad thing. The Appeals Division is mostly staffed with very knowledgeable people, supposedly the best that the IRS has to offer.

When you get to appeals, they will review your file. There may even be a telephone conversation with the appeals officer about the situation. They will review *everything*.

They may seek additional professional advice from other parts of the IRS if appropriate. It will be reviewed by a supervisor after the appeals officer makes their original decision.

They will notify you in writing of the decision of the appeals office. You will have a short period to agree or disagree. If you disagree, the IRS will go ahead with the collections process and issue a "Notice of Determination." You now have thirty days to do something or the IRS will issue levies, seize bank accounts, and begin other collection activities.

Collection Due Process Hearing

If you are getting pushed by collections and receive a "Filed Notice of Federal Tax Lien" or a "Proposed Levy or Actual Levy" and have not succeeded through the system to the Appeals Division yet you have the right to file a Form 12153 which is a request for a "Collection Due Process" hearing.

8 Payroll Tax Penalties, When The Irs Sends A Letter. - Www .., https://www.ralphcoutard.com/payroll-tax-penalties-when-the-irs-sends-a-letter/ (accessed November 10, 2017).

9 Ibid.

When you file a Form 12153, all collection activity must cease until the hearing. The hearing may take some months before it happens. The appeals officer should hold the hearing. You will have the chance to present to the hearing officer all of your evidence, forms, letters, call records and everything else that is pertinent to the case at hand. The hearing will normally be via telephone though some are in person.

United States Tax Court

Depending on the tax and the circumstances concerning the tax problem you can file a petition with the United States Tax Court. You may file Pro Se ("on one's behalf") without an attorney if you choose. I don't recommend it as the tax court has some procedures that you should follow. That being said, the Court is unusually lenient with Pro Se petitioners and will give you some latitude.

Some Pre Se clients win, but it is seldom. Most tax court cases get settled before ever going to court. If you have a "real" case, you can try it. But don't waste the court's time with frivolous petitions, they frown on it.

National Tax Payer Advocates Office

If you are getting nowhere with the IRS, you may want to consider meeting an expert at the National Tax Payer Advocates office. If Compliance or Collections are not playing by the rules, if you feel overwhelmed by the system and can't afford competent representation, the National Tax Payer Advocates office is an additional option and exists for exactly that kind of problem. Call them. Be prepared to send them everything. They stand outside the chain of command and have the authority to look at almost anything. They can't change a decision or action, but if you are right and being pressured by the IRS the Advocate's office knows who can fix things. That is their job to be an advocate of last resort for the taxpayer. To learn more about their services, go to https://taxpayeradvocate.irs.gov/.

It can be scary and intimidating, to say the least when you get a letter from the IRS stating that you made an error and owed penalties. Take a deep breath and don't worry. Many times you can win at getting the penalties abated. Remember to keep thorough records and proof of what you did so you can clearly and effectively state-your-case. If you stay the course, followup, persist and persevere without losing your temper you have a very good shot at success. Good luck!

TO DO:

- Water plants
- Clean booth
- Check voicemail
- Restock supplies
- Organize lobby

How to get commissioned staff to do the work you give them.

First Things First

The first question to ask, and it is covered in Chapter 1 in detail: is the worker an Independent Contractor or are they an Employee? If categorized as an employee, they are subject to FLSA and minimum wage. As an employee, they are subject to all the duties and responsibilities including following the rules set out in the employee handbook (covered in another section).

Employees

An **employee** that works partially for commissions is no different in concept than a wait staff that works for tips. Wait staff is paid a small amount, and the rest of their income comes from tips, but they are an employee. They are required to do "side work" such as clean the coffee machine and fold napkins for the next shift.

If they are unwilling to do their side work management will fire them, and they will no longer make the small hourly amount or the tips. Plus their fellow wait staff will make their life miserable because they will have to do the work because *it has to* get done to make the business run smoothly.

If they are an employee, part of the employee handbook should detail the duties that they are expected to do. Duties can be segregated by position, location, or shift or just referenced in the employee handbook to go to the daily or weekly schedule of duties outside of the commission earning activities.

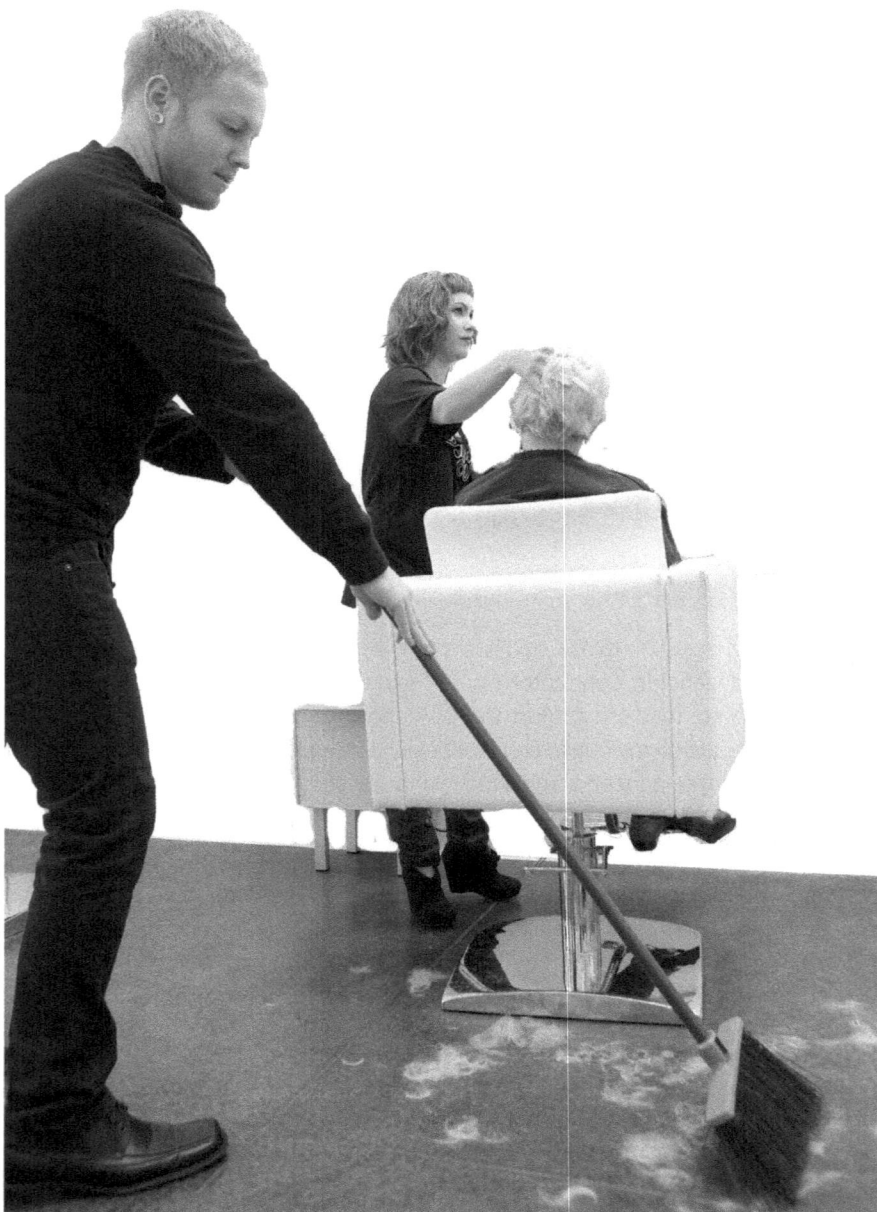

Create a daily plan of the day or a procedures manual.

You can create a daily "Plan of the Day." Activities and chores that get done each day, and who is to do them are listed and posted. In a restaurant, depending on the station, you are assigned to an area of responsibility which will determine the side work required for your shift. That station always has certain duties. If you work at that station, you know your duties in addition to taking care of customers.

It is smart to have a Procedures Manual that each employee is required to read, know and follow. It can be an addendum to your Employee Manual.

It's also a good idea to prepare an acknowledgment document, and ask each employee to sign it acknowledging that they have received and read the procedures.

The Procedures Manual will detail out each task and how it is accomplished. The more detail you can provide in the Manual the better. A general statement that says "straighten the supply room" leaves too much to interpretation. These procedures are written so that you can insist that they are done the way you want them done, every time by everybody.

Consistency will make it easier to run your company, and maintain the level of organization that you, the owner or manager, want. Your organization will not be subject to someone else's whim.

If the employees still don't want to comply, then your job is to either motivate them or terminate them for cause. The latter gets covered in another Section of this Guidebook. The former we will discuss later in this section.

Independent Contractors

Now, if they are an **Independent Contractor** what do you do? The key is in their title. There is a *contractor*. They have a contract with you do certain things.

Put the contract in writing. Make sure the contract spells out what additional duties that they must do under the contract. You can specify anything you want as long as it is not illegal for you to contract for those services. You obviously cannot have them do something that violates the law or could be ruled to be fraud.

> **A tip:** *You can contract that they will do their share of organization and cleanup of the work area as based on the "Plan of the Day," or you can have specific duties that they will accomplish on whatever basis you require.*

If they don't comply, then they are in breach of their contract. Of course, your contract should give you the right to terminate it at any time and for any reason of your choosing. It's your company. Your livelihood. Keep the control in your hands. If you do terminate a contract with an independent contractor, you will have to pay what they have earned through that point but probably not any longer. You need to have the dissolution of the contact as part of the contract.

Ideas to motivate employees and independent contractors.

Here are a few motivational techniques from other entrepreneurs that you can try with your employees whether commissioned or otherwise:

1. Gamify and Incentivize

Come up with creative ways to make the workplace fun. Many people respond positively to being rewarded for meeting certain goals or making games out of certain tasks. Healthy competition is always a good thing within the workplace. Offer prizes for goals met, selling certain product lines, or even amount of clients booked that week. Don't be afraid to think outside of the box! Remember to add incentives into your annual budget so you can afford to incentivize.

2. Let Them Know You Trust Them

Trust is an "evolving thing that ebbs and flows," says David DeSteno, a professor of psychology at Northeastern University and the author of The Truth About Trust (Get it on Amazon: https://www.amazon.com/The-Truth-About-Trust-Determines/dp/1594631239). And yet it's essential to boosting employee engagement, motivation, and candor, as stated in the Harvard Business Review article "Proven Ways to Earn Your Employees' Trust." (Read it here: https://hbr.org/2014/06/proven-ways-to-earn-your-employees-trust)

Without trust in your staff, workplace morale and productivity will suffer. Let employees know you trust and depend on them. A vote of confidence can go a long way. The Harvard Business Review wrote another great article on this topic recently called "Want Your Employees to Trust You? Show You Trust Them" published July 2017. They offer up seven questions you should answer to help determine if your team feels trusted. I've included them here:

1. Do I show my employees that I feel confident in their skills?
2. Do I show my employees that I care about their welfare?
3. Do I show my employees that I think they are capable of performing their jobs?
4. Do I give my employees influence over the things that affect them most on the job?
5. Do I give my employees the opportunity to take part in making job-related decisions that affect them?

6. Do I encourage my employees to take risks?

7. Do my words and deeds convey how much I trust my employees?[1]

Give up some of your control. Incrementally give away some of your control and give it to your employees. Your employees will take notice, and will take pride in knowing you believe they can handle it.

Share information with them. Keeping important information from them will breed distrust and suspect. Of course, while you don't want to tell them everything going on in the background of your company, sharing pertinent information that affects them promptly will allow your staff to gain confidence and trust. Transparency goes a long way.

Invest in your employees, and make a connection. Reward them by sending them to an educational class. Offer programs and flexibility for them to increase their education. Show support. Personally, connect with your employees. Get to know them and let them know about you. Let them know that you are one of them.

Create change where needed. Act on employees suggestions. Get more information on what they want and need. Take their complaints, put together a small group of employees to talk about it and come up with solutions. They will feel heard and validated, and trust will build.

Let them know you trust them to do the best job possible and they will very rarely disappoint you.

3. Set Smaller Weekly Goals

Rather than setting a goal to gross a billion dollars this year, instead break it down into digestible chunks with smaller weekly goals. Make your goals realistic and achievable. Saying you are going to make a billion dollars may be attainable and it may not.

Set your big goal for the year. Don't make too many big goals for the year or you may not have time to get to them.

Determine what steps you need to take to make that goal. Do you need to bring in a particular number of clients this year to make it happen? Do you need to sell a certain dollar amount of products or services? Do you need to hold payable events to meet your goal?

Break the steps into 52 parts - for each week of the year. If you want to grow your client base by 1000 new clients this year, then you need to bring in 84 new clients each month or 19 new clients each week. Does that seem doable? Bringing in a new

1 Want Your Employees To Trust You? Show You Trust Them, https://hbr.org/2017/07/want-your-employees-to-trust-you-show-you-trust-them (accessed November 11, 2017).

client does not guarantee recurring appointments so you may want to pad that number by 50% to give you a better chance of meeting your goal.

Create a weekly action plan. What steps do you need to repeat every week to meet your goal? Break it down even more.

> **Marketing Strategies**: Does it include marketing strategies like a weekly blog post highlighting a new technique or service, weekly emails highlighting a staff member ("Get to know <insert name>), or advertising a special?

> **Employee Goal Setting**: Incentivize your staff to sell a particular service or upgrade a service, set a retail sales goal, offer referral awards for the employee who brings in the most new clients. Get them talking outside of work for your business to bring in new clientele.

> **Partner with Another Local Business**: Affiliate your business with other businesses. Offer referral discounts in order to cross promote products/services. For example, approach a local fitness studio and create a cross relationship to offer a discount to any person who visits your business from theirs. Incentivize the owner of the business with a free or discounted service.

> **Hold a weekly event at your business**. Create a theme like Wine Wednesdays, Take Out Tuesdays, or Saturday Night Pajama Party. Invest in some decorations for your business, offer mini services and incentives to schedule services. Demo services that you want to push as well.

> **Volunteer**. While this may not be weekly, look for volunteer opportunities in the area to get your name out there. Are they any charities that hold annual gala's that you could set up tables and offer cosmetic touch-ups? Be creative. You'll be pleasantly surprised on how well it will be received.

These are simply a few ideas on how to set your weekly goals. Make sure you document them, set clear expectations, create a working calendar where you can visually check off your progress, and don't forget to celebrate the small goals you achieve each week. Reward the team for achieving the goal with an afternoon off, a party, etc. They will see that your goals are realistic and everyone benefits from working hard.[2]

4. Give Your Employees Purpose

Happy customers come from happy employees. Employees who are empowered are employees who find purpose and enjoy their jobs. How do you do that? Lighten up.

Micromanaged employees usually do not feel inspired or purposefully. Do you remember a time that you experienced micromanagement? It didn't make you want to

2 14 Highly Effective Ways To Motivate Employees | Inc.com, https://www.inc.com/ilya-pozin/14-highly-effective-ways-to-motivate-employees.ht (accessed November 11, 2017).

get up and eagerly go to work. Giving your staff more autonomy will breed happier employees and free up your time too (an added bonus).

Help them see the bigger picture: It's easy to develop tunnel vision on your job and forget about what you do affects the rest of the company. Hold an all-hands-on-deck monthly meeting to share what's happening in the company, highlight achievements, give an update on where they are with achieving the big picture goals.

Acknowledge their contributions: Take your monthly meeting and use some time to acknowledge individual contributions. Encourage your employees to share what they are working on with the rest of the company.

Even if your company is small, each person has an interest in something and may want to share it with the group. Something as small as re-organizing the product closet to make it easier for staff to get stock for their stations is something everyone will appreciate, so share it!

Trust your employees to be great: Take Dale Carnegie's advice on leadership and "give the other person a fine reputation to live up to." People rise to high expectations: it makes success feel imminent and attainable. (Source: https://www.forbes.com/sites/entrepreneursorganization/2014/04/08/empowered-employees-five-tips-for-giving-your-staff-a-sense-of-purpose/#e1bc47e5ae09)

Get them involved in some of the business operations like the interview process: Are you looking to hire a new stylist or massage therapist? Ask them to interview your potential new hire. Get the key players together beforehand, so you know what questions they will ask, and get feedback afterward. Also, if the interview includes a hands-on portion, have the interviewee perform the service on your employee and you, and compare notes. They will appreciate having a voice in who they could be working with in the future.

When you can give your employees a purpose, they understand the vision better and can execute it more strongly. By understanding their purpose and the purpose of the business, an employee is better able to understand how they fit into the big picture.[3]

5. Radiate Positivity

Let's face it. When you, the owner or manager, are in a bad mood, everyone is in a bad mood. You create a ripple effect that reverberates through your company. It can also continue past your walls to the people your employees interact with later in the day.

Here is a piece is I borrowed from the Harvard Business Review article titled *The Ripple Effects You Create as a Manager:*

3 14 Highly Effective Ways To Motivate Employees | Inc.com, https://www.inc.com/ilya-pozin/14-highly-effective-ways-to-motivate-employees.ht (accessed November 11, 2017).

"So what can you do to radiate positive, productive energy through employees at your workplace and out through their work-life networks? Here are a few ways:

Be a role model for work-life integration. Be open about your challenges and strategies for fitting together your work, family, and personal life. Let your employees see you as a whole person.

Appreciate others as whole people. The fact that everyone you work with has a life beyond work means that the team and the organization are embedded in a larger network of valuable relationships and shared goals.[4]

Appreciating the commitments that others have beyond work creates openness to looking for ways to create mutual work-life gains.

Be willing to experiment. Keep the focus on what your team or organization is trying to achieve and how each person can best contribute to those results. Ask people what would help boost their ability to achieve desired work results while also increasing their well-being beyond work. When employees are involved in designing and implementing solutions, their commitment to making them work is strong.

Offer socio-emotional support. Understanding of work-life challenges, sensitivity to how work can impact personal life, demonstrating respect, and offering encouragement go a long way in fostering positive relationships that help employees perform while keeping work-life conflict to a minimum.

Be an advocate for work-life integration in your organization. Promote the cause of work-life integration. Talk about why you believe it's important to recognize and respond to employees' work-life challenges. Share success stories and examples with other managers to help decision-makers in the organization understand how to provide work-life support."[5]

Happier employees are more productive, more innovative and more loyal to your business. Positively engage your employees and watch the ripple effect foster a happier work environment.

6. Embrace Transparency

I touched on this earlier. However, it's worth another mention. Transparency is important for your company's culture as it builds trust and loyalty in your staff and management. Keeping everyone in the loop allows for better communication and collaboration and overall leads to improved performance. How do you do it?

---

4   The Ripple Effects You Create As A Manager, https://hbr.org/2013/05/the-ripple-effects-you-create (accessed November 11, 2017).

5   The Ripple Effects You Create As A Manager, https://hbr.org/2013/05/the-ripple-effects-you-create (accessed November 12, 2017).

1. **Offer opportunities for candid conversations among your team**. Allow your staff to ask you the tough questions and answer them openly and truthfully. Your employees are the ones in the trenches doing the work, so they know when something is a problem or isn't working.

    A Tip: If they are apprehensive, you could have an anonymous submission box in the break room they can enter their question or concern, and you answer the questions from the box at the meeting.

Provide clarity along with access. Lots of data and information can be confusing so offer it in context and with clarity to avoid confusion.

>   **A Tip:** Put up a bulletin board in the breakroom and add updates for staff with information, goals, the status of open issues, and more.

2. **Don't wait to share the unfortunate news:** Employees don't like to be kept in the dark - would you? Share what you know when you know it, however, be reassuring and disarming. Open the lines of communication so they can learn from the experience and move forward maintaining the team environment. Thoughtfully sharing bad news goes a long way to build trust and can be a great learning experience.

Allowing for transparency in your business will make for better relationships, better alignment of each person's role, better solutions that are found faster, and better employee engagement.

8. Learn What Makes Each Employee Tick

Each employee works for different personal reasons. Learning what they can help you take steps to increase their work satisfaction and exceed your goals.

"For some employees, job satisfaction is directly related to compensation and financial rewards, healthcare, and other benefits, or training and growth opportunities. For others, intangibles such as company culture, management support and recognition, and peer camaraderie are what keeps them engaged and fired up about coming to work each day. But how do we figure out what matters most to each employee? The key to getting an answer to any question is to ASK IT."[6]

Take the opportunity in your employee one-to-one meetings to get a pulse on their needs. Compile the information together and see if there is a common need that perhaps you can give them. If it is too big to accomplish at the time, let them know you hear them and that it's on the radar to improve in the future. Ultimately, they will feel heard and valued as your employee, breeding loyalty, and harder working staff.

---

6   Knowing What Makes Your Employees Tick, https://www.predictiveindex.com/blog/knowing-what-makes-your-employees-tick/ (accessed November 12, 2017).

9. Prioritize Work-Life Balance

It is important to encourage employees to take vacation time. A culture that prioritizes work-life balance, yields increased productivity and overall happiness in the workplace. If your budget does not include vacation pay, offer incentives to earn free time. If they reach a goal, give them time off. They will greatly appreciate the time off.

10. Encourage Them To Lead

In this chapter, we've sprinkled in ways to give your employees the chance to lead by minimizing micromanagement, including them in interviewing processes and more. What else can you do to give them the chance to become a leader?

Here are 11 ways to groom leaders out of your staff I found in Inc. magazine in an article titled: How You Can Encourage Your Employees to Lead (Source: https://www.inc.com/lolly-daskal/how-you-can-encourage-your-employees-to-lead.html)

1. **Set the example.** To cultivate new leaders, you have to lead by example. Your habits and actions will set the standard for others and show others how it's done.

2. **Recognize their strengths.** Don't do anything on your own if it can be prevented, but recognize your employees' strengths and allow them to participate as much as they can. Don't take their talents for granted. Make it a point to talk individually with each member of your team to discuss their interests, strengths, and skills and encourage them to take charge.

3. **Let others make important decisions.** When you allow your employees to make important decisions, you are encouraging them to lead.[7] When they are empowered to make decisions that matter and can affect the organization, they see themselves as leaders.

4. **Give them more responsibility.** When you give an employee more responsibility, you are expressing faith in their abilities. The moment they take on more responsibility is the moment they can say, "Yes, I am stepping up." To cultivate more leaders, give them more to be accountable for--and let them know the price of influence is responsibility.

5. **Don't impose fear.** If you want to encourage more people to step up into their leadership, you have to lead without imposing fear. Great leaders inspire. Surround yourself with people of diverse perspectives, and establish a culture where they can disagree with you without fear.

6. **Help them plan their future.** To empower your employees, help them plan for the future. Get them to take responsibility for their career opportunities

---

7 Encouraging Your Employees To Lead | The Trocchio Advantage, https://trocchioadvantage.com/encouraging-your-employees-to-lead/ (accessed November 13, 2017).

through special assignments and special projects that take them down their chosen path.

7. **Trust them.** Trust is the glue that binds people together. To engage your people in leading begins by giving trust, and the only way to do that is to overcome the need to be in constant control. Ground your leadership in trust, and you set the example for those who come after to do likewise. [8]

8. **Help them grow.** Don't wait for prospective leaders to come to you--instead, you should approach them. Let them know what talent and qualities you see in them, and help them see how they can utilize their gifts for growth. The best way to engage more leaders is to show appreciation for who they are and help them stretch themselves. Show that you believe in them and give them opportunities to prove you right.

9. **Push their limits.** Sometimes people need a little push on their limits to avoid becoming stagnant. Without encouragement to stretch, people tend to stay in their comfort zone. It's your job to induce them into the kind of discomfort that produces growth.

10. **Respect them.** People tend to step up to the plate when you show them respect. If you want to empower your people to lead, you must respect them for who they are. The best leaders, go out of their way to boost their employees' self-esteem. As John Maxwell stated, when people respect you as a person, they admire you; when they respect you as a friend, they love you; when they respect you as a leader, they follow you.

11. **Praise and appreciate them.** If the actions of your employee inspire others to dream more, learn more, do more and become more, they are your leaders. Appreciate them for who they are and praise them for their leadership. Let them know how much their influence and inspiration mean to you and how they influence others." [9]

Encouraging your employees to lead is important and something you want to do because eventually as your business grows, you'll need a manager to run the day-to-day operations of your business while you step back and work on the strategies and growth of the business.

8   Ibid.

9   Encouraging Your Employees To Lead | The Trocchio Advantage, https://trocchioadvantage.com/encouraging-your-employees-to-lead/ (accessed November 13, 2017).

On the flip-side - be careful not to demotivate your employees.

As much as you should focus on motivating people, there may be some things you are doing unintentionally that could demotivate your employees. Here are some things to watch out for:

1. **Not fully respecting your employees as individuals**.

   Here are ways you may be disrespecting your employees: being chronically late for employee meetings; not returning their messages, or ignoring their suggestions for how to improve operations. These may seem like small things to an owner with weightier issues on his or her mind, but the reality is your employees resent them, and in turn, resent you. Remember, small things can make a big difference in one's feelings about work.

2. **Take credit for a project one of that which your employees did most of the work**.

   Taking credit away from anyone is guaranteed to make people angry. Good business owners and managers are secure enough to give full credit where it's due.

3. **Lose your temper**.

   While it may be human nature, people dislike being on the wrong end of a lost temper. Lost loyalty often follows lost tempers. As a business owner, you are no longer allowed to have outbursts when you are frustrated or angry. Your employees are always looking at you to gauge the feel and vibe of the business. Keep it together.

4. **Not standing up for your employees when under personal or professional attack**.

   A client receives a service, leaves seemingly happy, and calls the next day to complain. What do you do? Throw the employee under the bus or do you take ownership of it. Maybe your stylist had a bad day. It happens. Find out the details of what happened from the client's perspective, and before making a judgment or decision, talk to the stylist. While we like to believe that "the client is always right," that may simply not be the case. If the stylist was wrong, remember you hired them so take ownership of the error, and take steps to support and correct the issue with the employee. Everyone, even the client, will be happier.

5. **Be emotionally stingy**.

   Employees want to know they're doing a good job and are valued. But if they are doing well, simple words of encouragement are easy, inexpensive and can be motivational. If they never hear it, they won't last long.

While offering an Employee Handbook and Procedures Manual is the enforceable way to get your employees to do the work to keep the business running smoothly, a little finesse goes a long way. Be open. Be transparent. Be respectful. Be rewarding. All will go a long way in building trust and loyalty with your staff and ultimately to get the job done.

The Employee Handbook/Policy Manual

An essential component of your business makeup (pun intended).

An employee handbook or policy manual is an important communication tool between you and your staff. In the handbook, you detail everything that you want your staff to know how to work within your business. It sets an expectation for your new hire of what you expect from them as well as what they can expect from your company.

Additionally, legal information is also included such as an employee's' right-to-work, Family Medical Leave Act (FMLA), non-discrimination laws, and company policies: sick time paid holidays and earned vacation, uniform, working conditions, and more. It is a document that gets provided to every staff member upon hire.

Why should you create an Employee Handbook / Policy Manual for your salon or spa?

Consider this: All it takes is just one employee to cause you and your business problems. One.

Have these scenarios ever happened to you?

A stylist is repeatedly late for work. You talk to him about it, give him warnings that he could lose his job if he is continually late. But, he keeps being late. Do you have cause to fire him? Nope. What, you say? Why not?

An esthetician is not doing her daily tasks to keep her room clean, and it's noticeable. Her products have built up at the openings, supplies in her room are too low, she's not emptying her trash at the end of the day, the list goes on. You ask her politely to please keep her room sanitized, stocked, and organized. The next day, the same thing. And the next day. You ask her again...and again. You are fed up and want to fire her. Can you fire her for cause? No, you can't.

The answer is simple: You don't have a written policy that states that the stylist may be terminated if he is late a number of times, and you don't have a written task list that your esthetician has acknowledged receipt of that says she has to do these tasks daily or even at all. The possible result? Paying unemployment or even getting hit was a lawsuit.

Benefits for creating an Employee Handbook / Policy Manual.

While writing a handbook may seem like an insurmountable task, it's really not. There are lots of resources on the internet that can give you a great starting point, especially to handle including the legal jargon.

There are many benefits to having your own manual.

1. **It introduces your new hire to your company; it's values and culture.**

   Set a strong foundation by sharing your mission and vision for your company, allowing for a faster introduction to the level of standards you expect from them, as well as give them an easier sense of belonging.

2. **It elaborates for the employee what is going to be expected of them.**

   Roles, responsibilities, policies, and procedures for requesting time off, how to handle sick days, timekeeping, and more.

3. **It provides detailed information on what the employee can expect from you and management.**

   Leadership style, management best practices, and other legally required information is detailed in this section.

4. **It clearly communicates your specific company policies.**

   Standards of conduct, compensation, daily, weekly and monthly tasks that are required of your employee, uniform/appearance, arrival time, tools policy are some areas you can address here.

5. **It provides an easy way to share the benefits and perks your company offers**.

   Vacation pay, sick pay, general PTO days, health insurance, maternity leave, 401(k), gym membership, or any other benefits and perks are clearly listed as well as any eligibility requirements for each benefit.

6. **It keeps you compliant with state and federal laws**.

   Family Medical Leave Act (FMLA), Military Leave, Fair Labor Standards Act (FLSA), Occupational Safety and Health Act (OSH), are some of the laws you'll want to include here.

7. **It protects you against employee claims.**

   In chapter seven, we will review having your employee sign an acknowledgment document stating they received a copy of the handbook and reviewed it. This is your safety net if you are hit with a lawsuit from a terminated disgruntled employee.

If anything at all, number seven should get your attention and solidify why you need to have your own employee handbook.

What goes into an Employee Handbook / Policy Manual?

There are some things you **must** include in your handbook:

Equal Employment and Non-Discrimination policies.

"Per the U.S. Equal Employment Opportunity Commission (EEOC): The U.S. Equal Employment Opportunity Commission enforces Federal laws prohibiting employment discrimination. These laws protect employees and job applicants against employment discrimination when it involves:

- Unfair treatment because of race, color, religion, sex (including pregnancy, gender identity, and sexual orientation), national origin, age (40 or older), disability or genetic information.

- Harassment by managers, co-workers, or others in the workplace, because of race, color, religion, sex (including pregnancy), national origin, age (40 or older), disability or genetic information.

- Denial of a reasonable workplace accommodation that the employee needs because of religious beliefs or disability.

- Retaliation because the employee complained about job discrimination, or assisted with a job discrimination investigation or lawsuit."[1]

1 Unfair Treatment From Employers - Eeoc Home Page, http://www.eeoc.gov/employers/ (accessed November 14, 2017).

However, not everyone is covered under the EEOC.

1. To be covered under the EEOC for general discrimination categories listed above, a business must have a minimum of 15 employees for at least twenty calendar weeks. Otherwise, they are not covered.

2. To be covered under the EEOC for age discrimination practices, the business must have a minimum of 20 employees for at least twenty calendar weeks. Otherwise, they are not covered.

3. To be covered under the EEOC for pay discrimination practices, the business must have a minimum of 1 employee. So basically, as soon as you hire your first employee, you're bound by this law.

   Learn more about what may or may not be covered in your business, go to https://www.eeoc.gov/employers/coverage_private.cfm

   and

   https://www.eeoc.gov/employers/smallbusiness/requirements.cfm

Family Medical Leave Act policies.

"The FMLA entitles eligible employees of covered employers to take unpaid, job-protected leave for specified family and medical reasons with continuation of group health insurance coverage under the same terms and conditions as if the employee had not taken leave. Eligible employees are entitled to:

- Twelve workweeks of leave in a 12-month period for:
  - » the birth of a child and to care for the newborn child within one year of birth;
  - » the placement with the employee of a child for adoption or foster care and to care for the newly placed child within one year of placement;
  - » to care for the employee's spouse, child, or parent who has a serious health condition;
  - » a serious health condition that makes the employee unable to perform the essential functions of his or her job;
  - » any qualifying exigency arising out of the fact that the employee's spouse, son, daughter, or parent is a covered military member on "covered active duty;" or

- Twenty-six workweeks of leave during a single 12-month period to care for a covered servicemember with a serious injury or illness if the eligible employee is the servicemember's spouse, son, daughter, parent, or next of kin (military caregiver leave).[2]

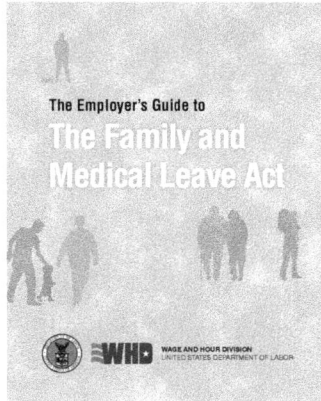

The Employer's Guide to
The Family and Medical Leave Act
WHD WAGE AND HOUR DIVISION UNITED STATES DEPARTMENT OF LABOR

Get the FMLA Employers Guide

Get the PDF version here:
https://www.dol.gov/whd/fmla/employerguide.pdf

Some States have more liberal rules for Family Leave than the Federal Policies. **If your State has policies about Family Leave they need to be incorporated in your handbook.** In all most all cases you will be required to follow the policies that give the most benefit to the employee.

Workers Compensation policies.

Workers' compensation is a form of insurance providing wage replacement and medical benefits to employees injured in the course of employment in exchange for mandatory relinquishment of the employee's right to sue their employer for the tort of negligence.[3]

Workers compensation policies vary from state to state. See the end of this chapter for a complete list. Find your state and click on the link to find out what you need to do.

Every State requires that you have workers compensation coverage, except Texas.

(Source: https://www.dol.gov/owcp/dfec/regs/compliance/wc.htm)

---

2 Family And Medical Leave Act - Wage And Hour Division (whd .., https://www.dol.gov/whd/fmla/index.htm (accessed November 14, 2017).

3 Workers' Compensation - Wikipedia, https://en.wikipedia.org/wiki/Workers%E2%80%99_compensation (accessed November 14, 2017).

ALABAMA

Department of Labor
Workers' Compensation Division
649 Monroe Street
Montgomery, AL 36131
(334) 242-2868 or 1-800-528-5166
www.labor.alabama.gov/

ALASKA

Department of Labor
& Workforce Development
Division of Workers' Compensation
1111 West 8th Street, Room 307
P. O. Box 115512
Juneau, AK 99811-5512
(907) 465-2790 or 1-877-783-4980
www.labor.state.AK.us
Commissioner.Labor@alaska.gov

ARIZONA

Industrial Commission of Arizona
Claims Division
800 West Washington Street
Phoenix, AZ 85007
(602) 542-4661
www.azica.gov

ARKANSAS

Arkansas Workers'
Compensation Commission
324 Spring Street
P. O. Box 950
Little Rock, AR 72203-0950
(501) 682-3930 or 1-800-622-4472
http://www.labor.arkansas.gov
asklabor@Arkansas.gov

CALIFORNIA

Department of Industrial Relations
Division of Workers' Compensation
455 Golden Gate Avenue, 2nd Floor
San Francisco, CA 94102-7014
(415) 703-5020 or 1-800-736-7401
www.dir.ca.gov/Contactus.html

COLORADO

Department of Labor and Employment
Division of Workers' Compensation
633 17th Street, Suite 400
Denver, CO 80202-3660
(303) 318-8700 or 1-888-390-7936
www.coloradolaborlaw.gov

CONNECTICUT

Workers' Compensation Commission
Capitol Place
21 Oak Street
Hartford, CT 06106
(860) 493-1500 or 1-800-223-9675 (Toll-
Free in Connecticut)
www.CT.gov/dol

DELAWARE

Department of Labor
Division of Industrial Affairs
Office of Workers' Compensation
4425 North Market Street
Wilmington, DE 19802
(302) 761-8200
www.Delawareworks.com

DISTRICT OF COLUMBIA

Department of Employment Services
Labor Standards Bureau
Office of Workers' Compensation
4058 Minnesota Avenue, N.E., 3rd Floor
Washington, DC 20019
(202) 671-1000
www.DOES.DC.gov
https://ohr.dc.gov/

FLORIDA

Department of Financial Services
Division of Workers' Compensation
200 East Gaines Street
Tallahassee, FL 32399-4220
1-800-342-1741
www.floridajobs.org

GEORGIA

Georgia State Board
of Workers' Compensation
270 Peachtree Street, NW
Atlanta, GA 30303-1299
(404) 656-3818 or 1-800-533-0682
www.dol.state.GA.us

GUAM

Workers' Compensation Commission
(671) 475-7033
www.dol.guam.gov/

HAWAII

Department of Labor
and Industrial Relations
Disability Compensation Division
Princess Keelikolani Building
830 Punchbowl Street, Room 209
P. O. Box 3769
Honolulu, HI 96812-3769
(808) 586-9161
www.labor.hawaii.gov

IDAHO

Industrial Commission
700 South Clearwater Lane
P. O. Box 83720
Boise, ID 83720-0041
(208) 334-6000
www.labor.Idaho.gov

ILLINOIS

Illinois Workers'
Compensation Commission
100 West Randolph Street
Suite 8-200
Chicago, IL 60601
(312) 814-6611 or 1-866-352-3033
(Toll-Free in Illinois)
www.state.IL.us/agency/idol

INDIANA

Workers' Compensation
Board of Indiana
402 West Washington Street
Room W-196
Indianapolis, IN 46204
(317) 232-3808 or 1-800-824-2667
(Outside Indianapolis)
www.in.gov/dol

IOWA

Iowa Workforce Development
Division of Workers' Compensation
1000 East Grand Avenue
Des Moines, IA 50319-0209
(515) 281-5387 or 1-800-562-4692
www.iowadivisionoflabor.gov

KANSAS

Department of Labor
Division of Workers' Compensation
401 SW Topeka Blvd, Suite 2
Topeka, KS 66603-3105
(785) 296-4000 option 9 or
(800) 332-0353 option 9
www.dol.KS.gov

KENTUCKY

Kentucky Labor Cabinet
Department of Workers' Claims
657 Chamberlin Avenue
Frankfort, KY 40601
(502) 564-5550 or 1-800-554-8601
www.labor.KY.gov

LOUISIANA

Louisiana Workforce Commission
Office of Workers' Compensation
1001 North 23rd Street
P.O. Box 94040
Baton Rouge, LA 70804-9040
(225) 342-7555
http://www.LAworks.net or
www.ldol.state.la.us/

MAINE

Workers' Compensation Board
27 State House Station
Augusta, ME 04333-0027
(207) 287-3751 or 1-888-801-9087
(Toll-Free in Maine)
www.maine.gov/labor

MARYLAND

Workers' Compensation Commission
10 East Baltimore Street
Baltimore, MD 21202
(410) 864-5100 or 1-800-492-0479
(Outside Baltimore)
www.dllr.state.MD.us

MASSACHUSETTS

Executive Office of Labor and Workforce Development
Department of Industrial Accidents
1 Congress Street, Suite 100
Boston, MA 02114-2017
(617) 727-4900 or 1-800-323-3249
www.Mass.gov/eolwd or
www.state.ma.us/

MICHIGAN

Department of Licensing
and Regulatory Affairs
Workers' Compensation Agency
7150 Harris Drive, 1st Floor
P. O. Box 30016
Lansing, MI 48909
1-888-396-5041
www.Michigan.gov/lara

MINNESOTA

Department of Labor and Industry
Workers' Compensation Division
443 Lafayette Road North
St. Paul, MN 55155
(651) 284-5005 or 1-800-342-5354
www.dli.mn.gov

MISSISSIPPI

Workers' Compensation Commission
1428 Lakeland Drive
P. O. Box 5300
Jackson, MS 39296-5300
(601) 987-4200 or 1-866-473-6922
www.mdes.MS.gov

MISSOURI

Department of Labor and Industrial
Relations
Division of Workers' Compensation
3315 West Truman Blvd., Room 131
P. O. Box 58
Jefferson City, MO 65102-0058
(573) 751-4231 or 1-800-775-2667
www.labor.mo.gov

MONTANA

Department of Labor and Industry
Employment Relations Division
Workers' Compensation Claims Assistance Bureau
1805 Prospect Avenue
P. O. Box 8011
Helena, MT 59604-8011
(406) 444-6543
www.dli.MT.gov

NEBRASKA

Workers' Compensation Court
P. O. Box 98908
Lincoln, NE 68509-8908
(402) 471-6468 or 1-800-599-5155
www.dol.Nebraska.gov

NEVADA

Department of Business & Industry
Division of Industrial Relations
400 W. King Street, Suite 400
Carson City, NV 89703
(775) 684-7260
labor.nv.gov

NEW HAMPSHIRE

Workers' Compensation Division
Department of Labor
95 Pleasant Street
Concord, NH 03301
(603) 271-3176 or 1-800-272-4353
www.nh.gov/labor

NEW JERSEY

Department of Labor
and Workforce Development
Division of Workers' Compensation
P. O. Box 381
Trenton, NJ 08625-0381
(609) 292-2515
lwd.dol.state.nj.us/labor/index.html

NEW MEXICO

Workers' Compensation Administration
2410 Centre Avenue, SE
P. O. Box 27198
Albuquerque, NM 87125-7198
(505) 841-6000 or 1-800-255-7965
www.dws.state.nm.us

NEW YORK

Workers' Compensation Board
20 Park Street
Albany, NY 12207
(518) 462-8880 or (877) 632-4996
www.labor.ny.gov

NORTH CAROLINA

Industrial Commission
4340 Mail Service Center
Raleigh, NC 27699-4340
(919) 807-2501 or 1-800-688-8349
www.labor.nc.gov

NORTH DAKOTA

Workforce Safety and Insurance
1600 East Century Avenue, Suite 1
Bismarck, ND 58503-0644
(701) 328-3800 or 1-800-777-5033
www.nd.gov/labor

OHIO

Bureau of Workers' Compensation
30 West Spring Street
Columbus, OH 43215-2256
1-800-644-6292
www.com.state.OH.us

OKLAHOMA

Workers' Compensation Court
1915 North Stiles Avenue
Oklahoma City, OK 73105
(405) 522-8600 or 1-800-522-8210
www.labor.ok.gov

OREGON

Workers' Compensation Division
350 Winter Street, NE
P.O. Box 14480
Salem, OR 97309-0405
(503) 947-7585 or 1-800-452-0288
www.Oregon.gov/boli

PENNSYLVANIA

Bureau of Workers' Compensation
Department of Labor and Industry
1171 S. Cameron Street, Rm. 324
Harrisburg, PA 17104-2501
(717) 783-5421 or 1-800-482-2383
www.dli.state.PA.us

PUERTO RICO

Industrial Commission
P.O. Box 364466
San Juan, PR 00924
(787) 781-0545
www.trabajo.pr.gov

RHODE ISLAND

Department of Labor & Training
Division of Workers' Compensation
1511 Pontiac Ave., Building 71-1, 1st Floor
P. O. Box 20190
Cranston, RI 02920-0942
(401) 462-8100
www.dlt.ri.gov

SOUTH CAROLINA

Workers' Compensation Commission
1333 Main Street, Suite 500
P. O. Box 1715
Columbia, SC 29202-1715
(803) 737-5700
www.llr.state.SC.us

SOUTH DAKOTA

Department of Labor and Regulation
Division of Labor & Management
700 Governors Dr., Kneip Bldg.
Pierre, SD 57501-2291
(605) 773-3681
www.dlr.sd.gov

TENNESSEE

Department of Labor
and Workforce Development
Division of Workers' Compensation
220 French Landing Drive
Nashville, TN 37243-1002
(615) 532-4812 or 1-800-332-2667
www.tn.gov/workforce

TEXAS

Department of Insurance
Division of Workers' Compensation
7551 Metro Center Drive, Ste. 100
Austin, TX 78744-1609
(512) 804-4000 or 1-800-252-7031
www.twc.state.TX.us

UTAH

Labor Commission
Division of Industrial Accidents
160 East 300 South, 3rd Floor
P. O. Box 146610
Salt Lake City, UT 84114-6610
(801) 530-6800 or 1-800-530-5090
www.Laborcommission.Utah.gov

VERMONT

Department of Labor
Workers' Compensation Division
National Life Building, Drawer 20
Montpelier, VT 05620-3401
(802) 828-2286 or 1-800-734-2286
www.labor.vermont.gov

VIRGINIA

Workers' Compensation Commission
1000 DMV Drive
Richmond, VA 23220
1-877-664-2566
www.doli.Virginia.gov

VIRGIN ISLANDS

Department of Labor
Workers' Compensation Administration
53 AB & 54 ABB Kronprindsens Gade
Charlotte Amalie, St. Thomas, VI 00803
(340) 776-3700 or 800-809-8477
www.VIdol.gov

WASHINGTON*

Department of Labor and Industries
Insurance Services Division
7273 Linderson Way, SW
Tumwater, WA 98501-5414
(360) 902-5800 or 1-800-547-8367
*mailing address
P. O. Box 44000
Olympia, WA 98504-4000
www.lni.WA.gov

WEST VIRGINIA

Offices of the Insurance Commission
1124 Smith Street
P.O. Box 50540
Charleston, WV 25305-0540
(304) 558-3386 or 1-888-879-9842
www.wvlabor.com/newwebsite/pages/
index.html

WISCONSIN

Department of Workforce Development
Workers' Compensation Division
201 East Washington Avenue
P. O. Box 7901
Madison, WI 53707-7901
(608) 266-1340
dwd.wisconsin.gov

WYOMING

Department of Workforce Services
Workers' Compensation Division
1510 East Pershing Boulevard
Cheyenne, WY 82002
(307) 777-5476
www.wyomingworkforce.org/Pages/
default.aspx

What else should you include in an Employee Handbook / Policy Manual?

This comprehensive list by The Balance categorizes your handbook for you and provides additional topics to consider that may not have been covered.

"Overview and Employment Relationship

- Introduction and Purpose of the Handbook

- Welcome Message from the President/CEO

- Company History

- Company Vision

- Company Mission

- Company Values

- Company Overall Goals

- Company Commitment to Employees

- Code of Conduct and Business Ethics

- Non-solicitation Policy

- Employee and Employer Confidentiality Agreement

- Non-compete Agreement

- Employee Handbook Disclaimer

- Employment Relationship: At Will Employment

- Employee Signoff Signifying Receipt of the Handbook, the At-will Statement, and Employee Acknowledgement That He or She Understands and Will Abide by the Contents

General Employment Information

- Equal Employment Opportunity Policy (article)
- Accommodation for People With Disabilities (article)
- Employment Eligibility
- Internal Employee Application Process
- Promotions
- Employment of Relatives
- Rehiring Policy
- Open Door Policy
- Personnel File Policy
- Access to Personnel Records
- Harassment and Discrimination
- Harassment and Discrimination Reporting Procedure
- Harassment Investigation Process
- Office Romances: Fraternization Policy

Attendance at Work

- Exempt and Non-exempt Employee Definitions
- Working Hours and Overtime
- Break and Lunch Periods
- Attendance Expectations and Policy
- Severe Weather and Emergency Closings
- Telecommuting Policy
- Termination When Unable to Work Policy.[4]

Workplace Professionalism and Company Representation

- Work Dress Code (provide images)
- Smoke-Free Workplace
- Drugs and Alcohol: Drug-Free Workplace
- Workplace Violence
- Weapons at Work
- Safety and Security
- Parking
- Workplace Visitors
- Conflicts of Interest
- Accepting and Giving Entertainment or Gifts
- Travel for Business Policy
- Mileage Reimbursement

Compensation and Benefits

- Payroll Information
- Compensation Schedule
- Recording Time Worked

---

4 Need To Know What Belongs In An Employee Handbook?, https://www.thebalance.com/need-to-know-what-goes-in-an-employee-handbook-191830 (accessed November 15, 2017).

Benefits

- Benefits Eligibility
- Health Insurance
- Dental Insurance
- Vision Insurance
- Group Life Insurance
- Disability Insurance
- COBRA
- Health Care Flexible Spending Account (FSA)
- 401(k) Plan
- Bonuses
- Workers' Compensation
- Unemployment Compensation
- Expense Reimbursement
- Educational Assistance
- Employee Assistance Program (EAP)
- Paid Legal Aid
- Supplemental Insurance
- Stock Options
- Employee Discounts
- Retirement

Employee Time Off From Work

- Paid Holidays
- Paid Time Off (PTO)
- Vacation
- Sick Leave
- Attendance Policy
- Family and Medical Leave (FMLA)
- Bereavement Leave
- Jury Duty
- Military Leave (USERRA)

Use of Company Equipment and Electronics

- Telephone Use
- Cell Phone Policy
- Company Tools, Equipment, and Supplies
- Computer and Internet Use Policy
- Blogging and Social Media Policy

Monitoring in the Workplace

- Email, Computer, Voicemail, Internet and Telephone Usage
- Video Surveillance and Physical Searches

Performance Expectations and Evaluation

- Performance Development Planning and Feedback Process
- Employee Conduct and Performance
- Immediate Employment Termination
- Progressive Discipline
- Conflict Resolution
- Complaint Procedure
- Employment Termination (article)
- Exit Interviews (sample questions)
- Return of Company Property"

(Source: https://www.thebalance.com/need-to-know-what-goes-in-an-employee-handbook-1918308)

An important side note: Your requirement to have workplace posters displayed in your place of business.

You are required to display workplace posters. At least you used to be required to display workplace posters. According to the Department of Labor, "Some of the statutes and regulations enforced by the U.S. Department of Labor (DOL) require that **notices be provided to employees and/or posted in the workplace.**"[5]

We suggest adding copies of the posters to your handbook. You can get them free on the Department of Labor website, or find them all in one place for free on our website: http://www.getpayroll.com/getpayroll-free-dol-posters/ On our website, you can copy and paste the small images right into your handbook.

Don't ever pay for DOL posters.

If you ever receive, and you will, an official looking notice in the mail that you are required to display the posters and you can buy them for $50-99, don't do it! They have always been and will always be free on the Federal and States DOL websites.

Some points to consider specifically for your Handbook for salon and spa employees.

If you are a service business, how do you want your employees greeting your clients?

What are your expectations of commission employees?

Are commission employees expected to clean their rooms and also clean the common area of the salon or spa?

Do you want your employees on social media during their workday?

Are your stylists and makeup artists allowed to take photos of their work at your place of business and post it on their personal Facebook pages, or perform services for income outside of working hours?

How are you collecting tips? Will you cash out at the end of the day or add their credit card tips to their paycheck?

Do the staff have to wear certain colors to work? What is their dress code? Does their hair have to be styled in a current or trendy fashion if they are a stylist? Do they have to wear the cosmetics that you sell at your salon to help advertise? (Keep in mind that if you are asking them to wear the products, you cannot make them buy the products to wear, but you can create a set of cosmetics they all can use daily to wear while at work.)

Decide on policies that are important to your business. Write them out and include them in your manual.

Resources

There are so many resources available to help you create an Employee Handbook/ Policy Manual from templates to what to include. Here are a few to get you started.

https://www.employee-checklists.com/res/pdf/EmployeeHandbook.pdf

http://spasalon.com/services/employee-handbook/

https://www.legalnature.com/lp/eh-295/Employee-Handbook?utm_source=-Google&utm_medium=ppc&utm_term=what%20should%20an%20employee%20handbook%20include&utm_campaign=Employee+Handbook+%7C+Ex&-fid=15365803&da=1&nl=1

https://formswift.com/employee-handbook

http://www.business-in-a-box.com/doc/employee-handbook-D712

https://www.shrm.org/resourcesandtools/tools-and-samples/pages/employee-handbooks.aspx

Wait! Next steps before providing your Employee Handbook / Policy Manual to your staff.

You are ready to distribute a copy of your brand new Employee Handbook. But wait. There are some steps to take. The Balance states it well:

"After you have prepared that employee handbook for your business, there are several more things you should do:

1. **Attorney review**. Have a labor attorney review the handbook for language, for conflicting or confusing language, and for legal issues. For example, your attorney can help you craft language that won't make employees think they have a job for life.

2. **Communication**. Make sure all current employees know about the handbook and that it is available to them. Give each employee a copy (make sure you get and keep a signature so you can show that all employees have received their copy).

3. **Put a copy up on the company website.** Remind employees about specific policies. In other words, make sure there's no way an employee can plead ignorance of the policies and procedures in the manual.[6]

4. **Implement**. Follow the handbook. Take action when you need to. Using the handbook to deal quickly with employee issues reinforces your intent to be fair and your intent to follow the handbook.

6 Why Does My Business Need An Employee Handbook, https://www.thebalance.com/why-does-my-company-need-an-employee-handbook-398090 (accessed November 15, 2017).

5. **Revise**. Re-visit the handbook periodically. Update policies that have changed (make sure you communicate the changes immediately!) and consider other changes to address issues that have come up. If you change a policy and you don't change the handbook, you're inviting legal issues."[7] If you make a change, get a new signature acknowledgment from every employee.

An excellent example of a salon/spa employee manual.

I scoured the web to see if I could find a company that was doing an excellent job at offering an employee manual, and I found one!

Luxe Salon and Spa offer a great example with which to base your own employee manual off. Take a look.

http://luxesalonaz.com/wp-content/uploads/2012/03/Luxe-Salon-and-Spa-Manual.pdf

I especially like the acknowledgment document in the beginning that states, "Please take time to read this cover-to-cover, print and return the signed Acknowledgement on the last page within 48 hours of receiving this."

And the text in the footer, "Luxe Salon & Spa at its option, may change, delete, suspend or discontinue parts or the policy in its entirety, at any time without prior notice. In the event of a policy change, employees will be notified. Any such action shall apply to existing as well as to future."

The management staff and owners are listed at the end of the letter. Having all management figures names at the signature of the letter is important so new hires are aware of who the decision-makers are for the business.

Consider adding all three components to your document.

7 Ibid.

At-Will Employment Agreement and
Acknowledgement of Receipt of Employee Handbook

Employer:

I acknowledge that I have been provided with a copy of the Boskin Robbitto (Waco) Bid D Ventures Employee Handbook, which contains important information on the Company's policies, procedures and benefits, including the policies on Anti-Harassment/Discrimination, Substance Use and Abuse and Confidentiality. I understand that I am responsible for familiarizing myself with the policies in this handbook and agree to comply with all rules applicable to me.

I understand and agree that the policies described in the handbook are intended as a guide only and do not constitute a contract of employment. I specifically understand and agree that the employment relationship between the Company and me is at-will and can be terminated by the Company or me at any time, with or without cause or notice. Furthermore, the Company has the right to modify or alter my position, or impose any form of discipline it deems appropriate at any time. Nothing in this handbook is intended to modify the Company's policy of at-will employment. The at-will employment relationship may not be modified except by a specific written agreement signed by me and an authorized representative of the Company. This is the entire agreement between the Company and me regarding this subject. All prior or contemporaneous inconsistent agreements are superseded.

I understand that the Company reserves the right to make changes to its policies, procedures or benefits at any time at its discretion. However, the at-will employment agreement can be modified only in the manner specified above. I further understand that the Company reserves the right to interpret its policies or to vary its procedures as it deems necessary or appropriate.

I have reviewed the Company Employee Handbook. I have read (or will read) and agree to abide by the policies and procedures contained in the Handbook.

By _____ Date _____
      Manager

By _____ Date _____
      Employee

JS (P a g e

The importance of an Employee Handbook/ Policy Manual Acknowledgement document.

You invest a lot of time into writing your Employee Manual, have it reviewed by your attorney, and make any necessary changes. It's ready to distribute. Wait.

It's vital to draft an Employee Handbook/Policy Manual Employee Receipt and Acknowledgement document that is provided to the new hire with the manual. Why? If the manual gets lost, there is no proof it was ever provided to them. This way, you're covered.

The employee should sign a document acknowledging receipt of the handbook. Whether they choose to read it is not your concern.

The moment the employee signs that document they are bound to follow the rules you have created for your company. If they do not, this is your legal safety net to terminate them without legitimate backlash. Of course, a terminated disgruntled employee may try anyway. However, you have that document as your proof.

A Tip: *Make sure you keep a copy in your locked personnel files.*

An acknowledgment document can be very simple or more complex. Either way, be sure to include these basic components:

1. Welcome message.

2. Instructions to read the Employee Manual, sign and date the document.

3. Due Date in which they must return to you the signed document.

4. Signed by all management and owners, so the new hire knows the decision makers of the company.

5. Statement at the bottom that says "To Be Placed in Employee's Personnel File."

We suggest keeping it simple and using a template like this one as your baseline.

EMPLOYEE HANDBOOK RECEIPT AND ACKNOWLEDGEMENT DOCUMENT

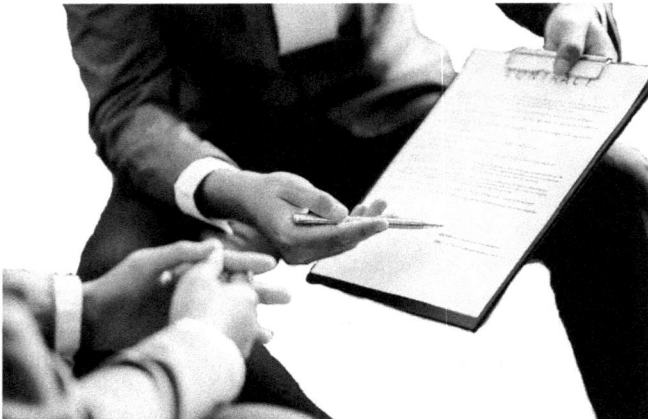

<business name>

Welcome to <business name>. We are excited that you are a part of our team. The purpose of the Employee Handbook/Policy Manual is, so we are both clear on our expectations of each other as we begin our journey of working together. This Handbook is a living document and will be updated annually. You will be asked to sign an acknowledgment of receipt each time it has been updated and redistributed.

As part of your employment, you are required to read the Employee Handbook/Policy Manual and return an acknowledgment of receipt.

Please take time to read this cover-to-cover, print and return the signed Acknowledgement on the last page within 48 hours of receiving this. [1]

We look forward to working with you. Welcome aboard!

1 Luxe Salon And Spa Manual, http://luxesalonaz.com/wp-content/uploads/2012/03/Luxe-Salon-and-Spa-Manual.pdf (accessed November 15, 2017).

<Owner Name(s), Title>

<Manager Name(s), Title>

I understand that it is my continuing responsibility to read and know its contents. I also understand and agree that the Employee Handbook is not an employment contract for any specific period of employment or for continuing or long-term employment. Therefore, I acknowledge and understand that unless I have a written employment agreement with <business name> that provides otherwise, I have the right to resign from my employment with <business name> at any time with or without notice and with or without cause, and that <business name> has the right to terminate my employment at any time with or without notice and with or without cause.[2]

I have read, understand and agree to all of the above. I have read and understand the <business name> Employee Handbook, and I acknowledge receipt of the <business name> Employee Handbook.

Signature _____

Print Name _____

Date _____

_____

For management:

Received by: _____

Date _____

To Be Placed in Employee's Personnel File

2 Sample Employee Handbook For Web - Northeast - Niqca, http://www.niqca.org/documents/Employee_Handbook.pdf (accessed November 15, 2017).

Semi-Weekly, Monthly, Quarterly, and Annual Payroll To-Do's

Ensuring your payroll and payroll taxes are correct and submitted properly, and on-time is crucial to keeping the IRS off your back. One mistake could cost you in IRS penalties. Depending on the size of your business, you may be a semi-weekly depositor or a monthly depositor of payroll taxes. You also have to submit quarterly and year-end reports to the IRS. It can become confusing.

We've created checklists to help you keep track as well as a payroll tax calendar, so you never miss a deadline.

Let's start with: what are you making tax deposits for?

You must make payroll tax deposits for:

- The amounts you withheld from employee pay for federal and state income taxes,
- The amounts you deducted from employee pay for Social Security and Medicare,
- The amounts you owe as an employer for Social Security and Medicare.[1]

---

1 How To Process Payroll And Payroll Taxes - The Balance, https://www.thebalance.com/how-do-i-process-payroll-and-payroll-taxes-398711 (accessed November 16, 2017).

- Plus, you have to make payment for:

- Federal unemployment tax on a regular basis.

- Payroll tax deposits to your state, and possibly your locality in addition to federal payroll tax deposits.

Payments are made using Form 8109 or using the IRS electronic filing system (EFTPS).

Are you a semi-weekly depositor or a monthly depositor?

On the Federal level.

The IRS determines the payroll taxes deposit schedule for employers based on their total gross Social Security/Medicare liability for the twelve-month period ending on the most recent June 30. This time period is called a look-back period (the time and amount used to which method you must use for your payroll tax deposit.).

The IRS says it's the total amount of employment taxes reported by the employer in the twelve-month period ending the preceding June 30. So, the payroll deposit schedule you use depends mostly on the amount of payroll taxes you owe, based on the past.[2]

On the State level.

The due dates State withholding or income tax will vary by state and are often determined by several factors. Some of the most common deposit frequencies are, but no limited to, monthly (due by the 15th of the following month), quarterly and next day. Some states will simply follow the same frequency as your federal withholding.

State withholding taxes do not have a wage base limit.

Determining your payroll tax deposit schedule.

- If you are a new employer and you did not have employees during this "look back" period, you are a monthly depositor.

- If your payroll tax obligation is less than $2,500 in a quarter, you can deposit these taxes with a "timely filed return" (assuming a Form 941).

- If your total payroll taxes for the "look back period" were **$50,000 or less**, you are a monthly depositor.

- If your total payroll taxes for the "look back period" were **more than $50,000**, you make deposits on the semi-weekly schedule.

2 How And When To Make Payroll Tax Deposits, https://www.thebalance.com/how-and-when-do-i-make-payroll-tax-deposits-398821 (accessed November 16, 2017).

When you should make your deposits.

- **Monthly Depositers**
  Under the monthly deposit schedule, deposit employment taxes on payments made during a month by the 15th day of the following month.

- **Semi-weekly Depositors**
  Under the semi-weekly deposit schedule, deposit employment taxes for payments made on Wednesday, Thursday, and/or Friday by the following Wednesday. Deposit taxes for payments made on Saturday, Sunday, Monday, and/or Tuesday by the following Friday.[3]

Semi-Weekly Deposit Schedule

If the payday falls on a:	Then deposit your taxes by the following:
Wednesday Thursday Friday	Wednesday
Saturday Sunday Monday Tuesday	Friday

If a deposit is required to be made on a day that isn't a business day, the deposit is considered timely if it is made by the close of the next business day. A business day is any day other than a Saturday, Sunday, or legal holiday.[4] **A legal holiday is any legal holiday in the District of Columbia only. State holidays do not apply.**

Legal holidays in the District of Columbia are:

- January 2—New Year's Day (observed)
- January 16—Birthday of Martin Luther King, Jr.
- January 20—Inauguration Day (every 4th year)
- February 20—Presidents' Day
- April 17—District of Columbia Emancipation Day (observed)
- May 29—Memorial Day
- July 4—Independence Day
- September 4—Labor Day
- October 9—Columbus Day
- November 10—Veterans Day (observed)
- November 23—Thanksgiving Day
- December 25—Christmas Day

It's important to make your deposits on time to avoid a penalty of up to 15%.

3 Publication 15 - Circular E, Employer's Tax Guide - 11 .., https://taxmap.irs.gov/taxmap/pubs/p15-010.htm (accessed November 16, 2017).

4 Publication 15 - Circular E, Employer's Tax Guide - 11 .., https://taxmap.irs.gov/taxmap/pubs/p15-010.htm (accessed November 16, 2017).

Quarterly Payroll To-Do's

Now it's time to focus on what you have due each quarter of each year. You pay at the end of the quarter for the previous quarter.

1. Form 941 - quarterly tax reports. (https://www.irs.gov/pub/irs-pdf/f941.pdf)

2. Federal unemployment tax (FUTA)

3. State income tax report

4. State unemployment tax (SUTA) and reports

A word about FUTA and SUTA tax.

The Federal Unemployment Tax Act (FUTA) and State Unemployment Tax Act (SUTA) provides unemployment compensation to those out of work. Employers pay by Federal and State unemployment taxes. Employees do not pay FUTA and SUTA tax; only employers do so. Refer to Publication 926 (2017), Household Employer's Tax Guide for more information.

FUTA tax is due by January 31st for the previous year.

If your tax liability exceeds $500, you have to pay FUTA.

If your tax liability does not exceed $500, you do not have to pay FUTA.

State unemployment taxes are based on a percentage of the taxable wages an employer pays. This taxable wage base varies by individual state and can be as low as $7000 and as high as $45,000.

Quarter	Quarter End Date	FUTA/SUTA Tax Due Date*
Q1 - January through March	March 31st	April 30th
Q2 - April through June	June 30th	July 31st
Q3 - July through September	September 30th	October 31st
Q4 - October through December	December 31st	January 31st

*If any of the due dates fall on a weekend, they are due on the following business day.

Year-End Payroll To-Do Checklist

The dreaded year-end. It comes every year during our busiest time of year. Doing payroll tasks doesn't help any either. Use this checklist to make your year-end tasks a little less painful.

W-2 Review and Update

☐ **CHECK TO ENSURE ALL EMPLOYEE INFORMATION IS CORRECT.**

- Name Changes
- Incorrect Social Security Numbers
- Home Address Changes

1099 Review and Update

☐ **CHECK AND MAKE SURE ALL INDEPENDENT CONTRACTOR DATA FOR 1099S IS CORRECT.**

- Name Changes
- Incorrect Social Security Numbers or EIN Numbers
- Business Address Changes

Order Enough W-2 and 1099 Forms

- If *you have not outsourced* your payroll make sure you have ordered enough W2 and 1099 forms and envelopes.

- *Remember, W-2s have to be submitted to the government by January 31st.*

- If *you have outsourced,* make sure your employees know how and where to download there W2s and your contractors their 1099s.

☐ Voided Check Processing

- Process any voided checks that have been accumulating during the year.

- Once you file the fourth quarter and year-end reports, it will be difficult and expensive to fix.

☐ Verify Your State Unemployment Rate and/or Disability Rate

- If they are wrong, update them and run a correcting payroll.

☐ Run Any Bonus Payroll

- Run your bonus payrolls with a check date in the current year.

- Record any payments made to employees or gifts that are deemed compensation before or with the last payroll.

☐ Review Any Fringe Benefits With Your Accountant

- If it is considered new this year to ensure they have been taxed properly.

☐ Cafeteria Plan Documentation

- Make sure you have your documents in your files for any cafeteria plan (Section 125) benefits that you offer. It may be difficult to get them if you get audited several years from now.[5]

☐ Plan Your Holiday Payroll

- Make sure you get the last payroll into the tax year you want it in.

☐ Third Party Sick Pay Information

- If you have third-party sick pay retrieve and record the information.

- You are required to make it part of your quarterly filings and in the employee's W2s (in many situations).

☐ Current Year Tax Tables

- If you don't outsource payroll make sure that you have current year tax tables in place.

- If not, update them and run a correcting payroll.

5 Your End-of-the Year Checklist — Getpayroll/simon, http://www.getpayroll.com/getpayrollblog/bp161220 (accessed November 17, 2017).

CALIFORNIA BUSINESS OWNERS: DON'T FORGET THIS ONE EXTRA TO-DO ON YOUR LIST.

☐ **California and FUTA Credit Changes**

- If you are in California make sure you understand the implication of the FUTA credit reduction for your state and what extra FUTA tax you are going to have to pay.[6]

Payroll Tax Due Dates Calendar

We scoured the web to find a thorough list that provides a complete monthly list of payroll tax due dates. The Balance website has an excellent article called: How to Set up a Yearly Payroll Tax Calendar, and we've provided their list here for your convenience.

General Payroll Tax Due Dates (Varies by Year)

Due dates for federal payroll taxes are as stated below except that deposits or reports are not due on a weekend or holiday. In any year when a due date falls on a weekend or holiday, the report or deposit is due on the next following business day. So, if a report is due January 15th, and that is a Saturday, the report is due January 17th.[7]

January

- January 15: Monthly Payroll Tax Deposit for December (if you pay monthly)

- January 30: Deposit Federal Unemployment Tax (FUTA) owed through December if $500 or more.

- January 31: Provide employees, contract workers with prior year wage and tax reports (form W-2 for employees; Form 1099-MISC for contract workers)

- January 31: File Quarterly Wage and Tax Report on Form 941 for the quarter ending December 31

- January 31: File Annual Unemployment Tax Report on Form 940 for the previous year

---

6 Your End-of-the Year Checklist — Getpayroll/simon, http://www.getpayroll.com/getpayrollblog/bp161220 (accessed November 17, 2017).

7 How To Set Up A Yearly Payroll Tax Calendar - The Balance, https://www.thebalance.com/how-to-set-up-a-yearly-payroll-tax-calendar-397319 (accessed November 17, 2017).

February

- February 15: Monthly Payroll Tax Deposit for January (if you pay monthly)
- February 28: Submit year-end employee transmittal forms (Form W-3) to Social Security Administration, along with all W-2s.
- February 28: Submit year-end contract worker transmittal forms (Form 1096) to Social Security Administration, along with all 1099 Forms.

March

- March 15: Monthly Payroll Tax Deposit for February (if you pay monthly)

April

- April 15: Monthly Payroll Tax Deposit for March (if you pay monthly)
- April 30: Deposit Federal Unemployment Tax (FUTA) owed through March if $500 or more.
- April 30: File Quarterly Wage and Tax Report on Form 941 for the quarter ending March 31

May

- May 15: Monthly Payroll Tax Deposit for April (if you pay monthly)

June

- June 15: Monthly Payroll Tax Deposit for May (if you pay monthly)

July

- July 15: Monthly Payroll Tax Deposit for June (if you pay monthly)
- July 31: Deposit Federal Unemployment Tax (FUTA) owed through June if $500 or more.[8]
- July 31: File Quarterly Wage and Tax Report on Form 941 for the quarter ending June 30

August

- August 15: Monthly Payroll Tax Deposit for July (if you pay monthly)

September

- September 15: Monthly Payroll Tax Deposit for August (if you pay monthly)

8 How To Set Up A Yearly Payroll Tax Calendar - The Balance, https://www.thebalance.com/how-to-set-up-a-yearly-payroll-tax-calendar-397319 (accessed November 17, 2017).

October

- October 15: Monthly Payroll Tax Deposit for September (if you pay monthly)
- October 31: Deposit Federal Unemployment Tax (FUTA) owed through September if $500 or more.
- October 31: File Quarterly Wage and Tax Report on Form 941 for the quarter ending September 30

November

- November 15: Monthly Payroll Tax Deposit for October (if you pay monthly)

December

- December 15: Monthly Payroll Tax Deposit for November (if you pay monthly).[9]

Avoid the risk of penalties and get prepared. Take the dates listed above and create your own calendar, so you are always aware of when your payroll taxes are due. Before you know it, it will become second-nature.

9 How To Set Up A Yearly Payroll Tax Calendar - The Balance, https://www.thebalance.com/how-to-set-up-a-yearly-payroll-tax-calendar-397319 (accessed November 18, 2017).

How to successfully create your brand and start building your social media presence.

Marketing sounds simple, right? You promote what you do to people - the consumer/potential customer - and they buy your service. Yay! So easy, right? Well, not so much.

What is marketing, really?

According to dictionary.com, **marketing [mahr**-ki-ting] is the total of **activities** involved in the **transfer** of goods from the producer or seller to the consumer or buyer, including advertising, shipping, storing, and selling.[1]

According to businessdictionary.com, marketing is The management **process** through which goods and services **move** from concept to the customer. It includes the coordination of four elements called the 4 Ps of marketing:

1. identification, selection, and development of a *product*,

2. determination of its *price*,

3. selection of a distribution channel to reach the customer's *place*, and

4. development and implementation of a *promotional* strategy.[2]

1 Fashion Marketing Flashcards | Quizlet, https://quizlet.com/185001096/fashion-marketing-flash-cards/ (accessed November 18, 2017).

2 Most Popular Business Terms Flashcards | Quizlet, https://quizlet.com/62158835/most-popular-business-terms-flash-cards/ (accessed November 18, 2017).

The American Marketing Association defines marketing as the **activity**, set of insti-tutions, and processes for **creating, communicating, delivering, and exchanging** offerings that have value for customers, clients, partners, and society at large.[3]

What do they all have in common? I've highlighted above the important points.

Activity and process are common words among the definitions and refers to the steps you take to get your business out there in the marketplace, so

1. people know about you,

2. what you sell (whether products or services), and

3. how to find you.

Transfer, move, deliver, exchange is the actual delivery of your product or service to the consumer. How do you get from point A to point B?

The four Ps of marketing.

The four P's of marketing, also known as a marketing mix, include *product, price, place, and promotion*. The idea is simple: find a way to select the right product, price it so consumers will want to buy it, place it in the marketplace, so it is easy to find and promote it to get the word out there that it's exactly what consumer needs right now.

Let's break it down into digestible chunks:

Product

Are you offering a tangible product and/or an intangible service to meet a customer need? It's vital for this step to know all the features your product or service has to offer, as well as it's unique selling proposition.

The key is to find a product/service that will meet an aspect of consumer demand, or compel them to believe they need it.

Take permanent eyebrows. Who would have thought to take tattooing to the next level and create a product and service to save women from having skinny or no eyebrows? That's an awesome product. It is a product that men, women, young and old could use. Women like to look and feel beautiful, but you already know that. Our eyebrows are key in expressing our emotions. If someone lost them due to over wax-ing or tweezing, illness, or they weren't born with full, lush brows, they will want this service. It is a unique product AND service proposition that can be sold B2B and through to the consumer.

---

3 Definition Of Marketing, https://www.ama.org/AboutAMA/Pages/Definition-of-Marketing.aspx (accessed Novem-ber 18, 2017).

At this point, you also need to start identifying who your target market or customers are going to be?

Price

What are you going to price your products and services? You will want to identify perceived value rather than what you think it should be priced. As a business owner, it's easy to get swept away about how fantastic your idea is so of course others will think the same. Reality check: that's never the case. Consumers want to pay the least amount for the most value. It's become more and more obvious with the creation of Groupon and Living Social sites. If a customer can get a service for practically nothing, they will choose that over your product or service. While there are some exceptions, this is more the norm today than in years past.

Know your cost to produce the product or service and mark your product/service up accordingly so you can make a profit. You will need to take into account overhead costs, advertising/marketing costs, and employee costs to price your item or service.

Do your research! Look at the area you are living, where your business is located, what is the median income for your area? Check out other businesses that you view as viable competitors. Price your products and services closely to what you find.

Place

Where will your product or service be sold and how do you plan on getting it to market? If you are a salon owner, you'll want to retail your products at your business, create an online store to sell your products online, and perhaps even look at local boutiques to sell your product line in their stores and split the profit.

If you are marketing a service, you will perform the service at your business location. You can also do on-location work, mobile services, volunteer at events to show off your work, sell gift certificates for services online, to name a few. The idea is to get creative in getting it into consumers hands, so they buy it.

Promotion

Brand is a key player in promotion. Promotion is what you will do to get the word out about your business, products, and services. Advertising, public relations, and other strategies fall into promotion.

The key in promotion is to educate the consumer on

- what you have,
- how it works,
- why they need it,
- why they should pay a certain price for it, and
- why they should buy it from you.

There are so many ways to promote your business. The key is to research which ideas would work best for your business.

There is a product lifecycle.

The product life cycle is the time that you have an idea for a product; the product is developed, brought to market, and finally, removed from the market to be replaced with another one.

There are four stages of a product lifecycle that I'll cover briefly.

1. **Introduction:** This stage is when you are first bringing the product to market. It can be the most expensive phase of the life cycle because you are putting a lot of marketing efforts out there while getting little return. This will change over time.

2. **Growth:** This is the favored stage of the life cycle as it is when the speed that your company is gaining positive returns is growing quickly. Economies of scale tip in your favor. Less is needed to market while profits are rising.

3. **Maturity:** Your product is reaching its peak regarding sales and performance. This is the time to work to maintain your status in the marketplace while working to beat your competitors who have joined the race. Product improvements and modifications are made during this stage to maintain the level of product success and competitive advantage.

4. **Decline:** The final stage of the product lifecycle. Sales start to decline, and there could be several reasons including market saturation and shrinkage. All the customers who should buy have bought it, or the need for the product has diminished in the consumer's eyes.

Even though your product or service will hit the decline phase, you have the opportunity to switch your market and may find less expensive production costs to keep your product flourishing in the market longer. You also have the opportunity to update your product and re-launch it in the market to begin the life cycle stages all over again.

How can this be seen in the beauty industry?

For hair salons, there are new techniques for cutting and styling that are developed every year. There are new ways to color hair that is trendy, and everyone wants it. Styles will continue to come and go, and these styles are "products" in the life cycle. Each year you market the trendy color or cutting technique, new product launches or new equipment, all of which can be viewed as a product in the life cycle.

For day spas, I've seen (having been an esthetician for almost 30 years), new facial techniques that developed, new seasonal facials, new peels, and the rise in vegan-type and organic facial products. There is also new machinery you may purchase and add as a service - the Hydrafacial, microdermabrasion, skin tag removal, and more. All of these are considered "products that will run its course in the life cycle."

Some products/services will have long life cycles, like microdermabrasion. It's been around for years, has noticeable results, and continues to improve.

> When microdermabrasion first entered the market, it was with crystals, the machines were very large and expensive, and the service you charged was expensive as it was considered cutting edge (the ***introduction*** stage).

> Microdermabrasian became "the service" for pigmentation issues and anti-aging issues - two skin conditions that everyone has to deal with as they get older - so everyone wanted it (the ***growth*** stage).

> Now, machines offer diamond tip alternatives, partnered with red or blue light therapy, machines are affordable, and the prices have changed to be reasonable for the consumer (the ***maturity*** stage).

> We have yet to get to the point for the ***decline*** stage, even with the introduction of microdermabrasion like service like the Hydrafacial.

The importance of branding.

To brand your business, you first need to decide what feeling or vibe you want your salon or spa to have. Are you edgy or are you whimsical? Are you contemporary or are you classic?

Choose your colors wisely and use them in every aspect of your decor and marketing materials.

Colors and fonts subconsciously tell your customers what they can expect when they enter your business. And we haven't even started talking about the words you'll use. Do you want to be seen as contemporary and cutting edge, or do you want to be seen as bold and vivacious? Feelings can be captured with color. The key is to look at yourself and your vision for your company, and select colors that not only show your personality but what you want to communicate to your customers as well.

Color and Emotions Examples

For more information on color, creating color combinations to communicate particular feelings, including percentages of color to use to create that feeling, go to coschedule.com: https://coschedule.com/blog/color-psychology-marketing/, for The Know It All Guide To Color Psychology In Marketing + The Best Hex Chart. You can download several resources on color included the chart below, color and word associations, and 33 complete color schemes for color psychology in Marketing.

COLORS BRING
Emotion

BLUE

(+) TRANQUILITY, SECURITY, INTEGRITY, PEACE, LOYALTY, TRUST, INTELLIGENCE

(−) *COLDNESS, FEAR, MASCULINITY*

TURQUOISE

(+) SPIRITUAL, HEALING, PROTECTION, SOPHISTICATED

(−) *ENVY, FEMININITY*

GREEN

(+) FRESHNESS, ENVIRONMENT, NEW, MONEY, FERTILITY, HEALING, EARTH

(−) *ENVY, JEALOUSY, GUILT*

YELLOW

(+) BRIGHT, SUNNY, ENERGETIC, WARM, HAPPY, PERKY, JOY, INTELLECT

(−) *IRRESPONSIBLE, UNSTABLE*

PURPLE

(+) ROYALTY, NOBILITY, SPIRITUALITY, LUXURY, AMBITION, WEALTH

(−) *MYSTERY, MOODINESS*

PINK

(+) HEALTHY, HAPPY, FEMININE, SWEET, COMPASSION, PLAYFUL

(−) *WEAK, FEMININITY, IMMATURITY*

RED

(+) LOVE, PASSION, ENERGY, POWER, STRENGTH, HEAT, DESIRE

(−) *ANGER, DANGER, WARNING*

ORANGE

(+) COURAGE, CONFIDENCE, FRIENDLINESS, SUCCESS

(−) *IGNORANCE, SLUGGISHNESS*

BROWN

(+) FRIENDLY, EARTH, OUTDOORS, LONGEVITY, CONSERVATIVE

(−) *DOGMATIC, CONSERVATIVE*

TAN

(+) DEPENDABLE, FLEXIBLE, CRISP, CONSERVATIVE

(−) *DULL, BORING, CONSERVATIVE*

GOLD

(+) WEALTH, WISDOM, PROSPERITY, VALUABLE, TRADITIONAL

(−) *EGOTISTICAL, SELF-RIGHTEOUS*

SILVER

(+) GLAMOROUS, HIGH TECH, GRACEFUL, SLEEK

(−) *INDECISIVE, DULL, NON-COMMITTAL*

WHITE

(+) GOODNESS, INNOCENCE, PURITY, FRESH, EASY, CLEAN

(−) *ISOLATION, PRISTINE, EMPTINESS,*

GRAY

(+) SECURITY, RELIABILITY, INTELLIGENCE, SOLID

(−) *GLOOMY, SAD, CONSERVATIVE*

BLACK

(+) PROTECTION, ELEGANCE, DRAMATIC, CLASSY, FORMALITY

(−) *DEATH, EVIL, MYSTERY*

A word about Fonts.

Typically, you want to select fonts that will share your brand but also that are legible. There are tons of really cool and funky fonts on the market today that you can purchase and download to your computer that goes beyond what is supplied in your design software programs.

Adobe has their Type Tool Kit with their additional font options to download. Some are free, and some are a small fee. They automatically download into Adobe products for immediate use.

Another great resource is creativemarket.com. Here you'll find the newest fonts created for the market today. You can purchase a single font or a bundle to offer up different marketing opportunities.

Here are a couple of examples from their website. Click on each to go to their web pages on the creative market website.

Start with two fonts.

I suggest starting with two fonts:

>**One font is used for your first level headlines or H1s.** This is the eye-catching font to you use with your tagline to grab the consumer's attention. These types of fonts are great in print, but they are not web friendly. Using them in your website or blog posts will mean creating images out of your headlines and inserting them into your layouts.

>**One font is something simple and easy to read, like Arial or Helvetica.** These fonts are rounded and very easy to read. Arial and Helvetica are used both in print and as a web font. Be sure to select a font that is both print and web friendly.

Important marketing materials every salon and spa should have.

There are the basics that every small business owner should have. The same holds true for your marketing materials. Keep it simple. Don't go overboard creating all sorts of marketing materials until you need them. It's a waste of resources. Start with these three marketing pieces:

1. **Website**

   According to Forbes.com, there are three reasons why websites are vital to small businesses. Online visibility is crucial in today's market. Most consumers use the internet as their first step in shopping. Gone are the days that a yellow page ad was all you needed. Now, websites are crucial to business success.

   a. **First Impressions Count:** Your website presence will help consumers decide whether they want to visit your business or not. If your website is basic, they will think your business is basic. Make it count.

   b. **Window Shopping Isn't What It Use to Be:** Not only is your website important but having a presence in search engines and review sites are vital too. Good

SEO (search engine optimization) will help you get higher in the Google rankings so your website can be found. The more review sites you are on will also go a long way in getting you noticed on the web.

c. **No Website Means Losing Business:** No presence on the internet means you will not get found by consumers. It's bad for business not to have a website today. Getting found means having a website.

2. Business cards

Business cards, really? In the digital age, are business cards still necessary? Yes, they are. According to thebalance.com, there are Seven Reasons You Still Need Business Cards.

a. Digital devices, such as smartphones, are everywhere, but that doesn't necessarily make it any easier or faster to give someone your business contact information.[4]

b. Some people do not own digital devices.

c. Business cards have no downtime.

d. Business cards provide a legitimacy to your small business.

e. Business cards provide promotional opportunities.

f. Business cards are necessary to make deals in some situations and/or cultures.

g. Business cards facilitate networking.

I particularly agree with the idea that business cards provide legitimacy to your company. How many times have you talked to someone about their business and then asked for a business card? How do you feel about them when they say they don't have one. They lose some credibility, don't they? Business cards should be an extension of your hand when networking and promoting your business. They are here to stay for the foreseeable future.

What should you include on your business card? Keep it simple. I am a fan of keeping one side blank so the recipient of the card can make notes on it for future reference.

The front of your business card should reflect your brand image with logo, fonts, and colors that are consistent with your brand, and:

1. Business logo
2. Business name
3. Your name
4. Business Address
5. Business Phone
6. Business Website
7. Business Email
8. Tagline

4 7 Reasons You Still Need Business Cards - The Balance, https://www.thebalance.com/why-use-business-cards-2947920 (accessed November 18, 2017).

3. Services Brochure with pricing

Brochures are an extension of your brand image. Brochures provide detailed visual information about your products and services. There are two types of brochures: hand-held to give to your customer directly, and an e-brochure to communicate to the masses. I recommend both.

    a. Things to include in your brochure:

- » Business logo
- » Business name
- » Business Address
- » Business Phone
- » Business Website
- » Business Email
- » Tagline
- » Listing of Services with descriptions and prices.

- » Listing of Products your retail, and link to your online store (if you have one).
- » Use descriptive words but do not exaggerate or use words they won't understand.
- » Include a call-to-action. The simplest offer can get people to take action.

Resources:

Vistaprint.com for printed materials.
Moo.com for printed materials.
Squarespace.com for website design. (Better templates)
Wix.com for website design.
Fiverr.com for anything and everything.

> **Tip:** *Sites like those listed above have design templates created for industries. If you do not know how to design your own print layouts in photoshop or similar software or web design in Wordpress, don't simply select a design from your industry. Remember, everyone will be doing that! Pick something else and tweak it to be your brand. Replace pieces of their layouts to customize it to be your own.*

If you know how to do website design, use WordPress. WordPress has awesome templates for add-ons to make your website more dynamic.

Last notes about your printed collateral.

- Don't use flimsy paper.
- Don't print them on your printer.
- Don't print them in black and white.

- Get them printed professionally.
- They are advertisements for your business and should represent the quality you provide in your business.

Using social media to grow your business.

Build a Brand on Social Media

There are key things you should do when building a brand on social media. As mentioned, you need to have a consistent brand for your business. Your logo, tagline, color scheme, and fonts should accurately represent your business in every piece of marketing materials including your website. Be consistent with your brand image. *Prospects will begin to recognize it through social media.*

Select social media sites that will represent your business and gather customers that share them. Are you a B2B or B2C business?

If you're B2B, LinkedIn should be on your radar.
If you're B2C, Facebook and Twitter may be better.

Will YouTube, Instagram, and Pinterest help propel your business forward? Check your competitors. What are they doing?

Salon and spa owners should consider using Facebook, Twitter, YouTube, Instagram, and Pinterest for your business.

Facebook

Every business should have a business Facebook page. A business Facebook page allows people to Like your page. Your brand image should be consistent with your images you add to your page. It should be, in essence, a mini-website. They should be able to find any information about your business on your page. You do not want Facebook users to have to request to join your group; they will most likely turn away and find someone. One of the keys to social media is quick bite-sized consumption and action. Making things as easy as possible is one of your social media goals.

Utilize add-ons with Facebook. Frame in your online appointment calendar so clients can book appointments right from Facebook. Link Twitter. Whatever posts on your Facebook page will auto post to Twitter. Add a tab for youtube videos. There are many add-ons on Facebook that you can use to maximize your exposure.

Engage your Facebook fans with contests and giveaways. Do some Facebook Live videos - Daily Dose, Beauty Bytes, Go Live...come up with any catchy phrase that will become your statement for Facebook Live events that your followers will come to learn and know.

Facebook Live

Salons I love on Facebook utilize Facebook Live quite a bit. Creating a daily show of your business with stylists in action is a great way to build interest and intrigue your business. You can show off your employee skills and techniques, talk about specials you are having, and if you have any openings with particular stylists.

You can also use Facebook Live to educate. Show a demo style, makeup application, or skin care service. Seeing your services performed live in action and learning something too is a great way to get customers into your business. You can interact with your customers, answer their questions, which will ultimately gain interest for your business. Keep them short - 5-10 minutes tops.

Facebook Ads

If you are growing your business, consider Facebook Ads. You can scale your ad directly to your demographic and area so only those in the areas you are looking for will see the ad. Drive traffic to your website, get more Likes on your Facebook page, schedule more appointments or sell a product. Remember to view your data after a promotion so you can tweak your messaging closer to what works and doesn't work.

Twitter

Twitter is about engagement. It's great to shout out a quick and short message and link to an image or video. This is great advertising to show off your work. Twitter, like Facebook, makes it easy to like and share tweets expanding your reach. Start your own hashtag and have a contest for those to post using it.

YouTube

In the beauty industry, it's vital to show off your work. That's how people know the quality of work you can do, and it almost effortlessly gets you new business. YouTube is an excellent way to do that. Facebook Live is great for short videos, but YouTube is excellent if you want to share a tutorial on how to do something like "How to

Style Your Wedding Hair on a Budget." Or, "Check Out Our Take on the New Copper Color Trend," and show segments of your stylists doing the color in action, plus several after looks and how you got there. It all builds credibility for you and your business. Hair styling, hair cutting, hair coloring, demonstrating a new facial machine, makeup application, are all ideas that you can exploit on YouTube.

Instagram

Photos, photos, and more photos. Before and afters. Step-by-steps, Variations of the same style or colors, finished products, stylists in action, are all ideas that should be documented on posted on all of your social media but especially Instagram. Share your work through photos and build your following, not to mention your credibility.

Pinterest

Pinterest is also a photo sharing site, but it's more about curation, gathering photos to create themed storyboards. This is a great place to share the current and upcoming trends, styles you love, and more. It gives your followers a look inside to what you like. It's a great place to marry beauty with other aspects that may follow suit.

LinkedIn

LinkedIn is primarily a B2B - business to business - social networking site. It is a great idea to post your personal profile page on LinkedIn is if you want to make industry contacts, or if you are looking to meet other people in your industry. If you are looking for customers, it's not the number one site to use for that.

There are so many other sites out there that you could jump into, however, keep in mind that you have to work to maintain them and keep them current continually. Who has time for that? Instead, pick the social media sites that will give you the most bang for your buck, and spend your time wisely.

Check out Social Media Marketing For Salons for additional tips at https://blog.wishpond.com/post/89814626545/social-media-marketing-for-salons-21-tips-and

Get some help.

Doing all the marketing on your own can be a daunting task. There are numerous marketing campaign systems out there that can help you create professional looking campaigns to gain customers. Check out these resources and see if any might work for you:

https://www.wishpond.com/explore-wishpond/
http://saloniq.com/salon-marketing/
https://worldwidesalonmarketing.com/
http://get.promorepublic.com/deluxe-beauty/

There is so much more to marketing and branding your business. However, we hope this gives you a launching point to get going with properly branding your business. Establish yourself as a thought leader and educate while sprinkling in sales. Be consistent, and you'll see your business grow and thrive.

Interviews: Do's and Don'ts

Also, questions you should avoid and what you can ask instead.

Have you given thought as to the questions you ask a potential employee during an interview? As a small business owner, it can be both stressful and intimidating to interview. What questions should you ask? How much information do you give out about yourself and your business? It can be daunting.

Believe it or not, there are things you want to consider when interviewing candidates for your job. There are questions you can ask and ones you should avoid. We believe it is very important to know what to ask in an interview and what not to ask. During every job interview, there is certain information you are looking to obtain through friendly banter with the potential candidate. However, some questions you may be currently asking interviewees could come across as a little too friendly and may be perceived as potential discrimination.[1]

On a federal level, there are many areas you want to steer clear.

1. "Race, color, national origin, sex, and religion (covered under Title VII of the Civil Rights Act of 1964);

2. Age (covered under the Age Discrimination in Employment Act);

---

1 10 Interview Questions You Can't Ask And 10 Legal .., http://www.getpayroll.com/payroll-academy /2017/5/11/10-interview-questions-you-c (accessed November 19, 2017).

3. Disability (covered under the Americans with Disabilities Act);

4. Results of genetic testing (covered under the Genetic Information Nondiscrimination Act).

In addition to the characteristics protected under federal laws, various states and local jurisdictions add other characteristics protected by law. Such characteristics include but are not limited to sexual orientation, gender identity, service in the military, veteran status, ancestry, arrest record, marital status, and whether someone is a victim of domestic violence."[2]

Here are some do's and don'ts for successful interviewing and avoiding legal trouble.

Interview best practices

- Read the resume before the interview. It's important to be prepared and know who with whom you are speaking.

- Schedule the same amount of time for each candidate. It will keep you on track and focused on the questions you want to ask.

- Ask the same questions to every candidate to avoid discrimination issues.

- Create a word document with each question and space to write their answers underneath each question. Consistency among interviews saves you headaches and time.

- Do not write on the resume. Notes that are vague or ambiguous could be misconstrued.

- Limit small talk. You may inadvertently ask a question that the candidate may view as discriminatory.

- If you include a test in your interview, be sure to have a printed activity sheet that is the same for every candidate. Ensure the test is the same for everyone.

- Avoid working interviews unless you plan on paying for their time. Be sure the candidate is aware that it is a working interview and the amount of time that she will be required to perform. We have heard of several cases where a candidate did a working interview and then tried to claim unemployment. And, they won. It happens.

- Remember to use some soft skills. The interviewee is nervous. Show some empathy and understanding. After all, we've all been there.

2 Bringing On New Employees? Don't Let Applications .., http://www.hrhero.com/hl/articles/2017/09/29/bringing-on-new-employees-dont-let- (accessed November 19, 2017).

Five interview landmines to avoid.

As a business owner or manager, you are so busy with your daily tasks of running and managing your business; it's easy to forget to prepare for your interviews. Monster.com breaks them down for us and provides ways to avoid them.

1. "Fail to define a clear picture of the job requirements.

   a. Do you have a clear picture in your mind of the performance you want to see from the position you are filling? Are you and the other people interviewing candidates in agreement on what you are looking for in the person you hire?[3]

2. Fail to create a scorecard for the interview

   a. Create an interview scorecard that lists the key accomplishments and skills you want in the person you hire. You might have seven criteria (sales skills, organizational skills, leadership abilities, etc.) for which each interviewer scores the candidate from 1-5.

3. Fail to ask open-ended, accomplishment-oriented questions.

   a. If you had to walk into an interview right now, with zero preparation, could you ask good interview questions and learn everything necessary to make a judgment about the candidate?

4. Fail to listen

   a. In most interview situations, you should be asking open-ended questions, listening, asking a follow-up question, listen, and then repeating the process.

5. Fail to do a post-game debrief

   a. Immediately after everyone has interviewed the candidate, or as quickly as possible after that (within 24 hours at the most) meet with the other interviewers to do a post-game debriefing to discuss your impressions."[4]

Common Interview Questions

In every interview, there are common sense and very common questions that almost every interviewer asks. We've listed them here.

1. Tell me about yourself.

2. Tell me about your top strength and weakness.

3. What would you consider your greatest career accomplishment?

3 5 Interviewing Mistakes Hiring Managers Should Avoid .., https://hiring.monster.com/hr/hr-best-practices/recruiting-hiring-advice/intervi (accessed November 19, 2017).

4 5 Interviewing Mistakes Hiring Managers Should Avoid .., https://hiring.monster.com/hr/hr-best-practices/recruiting-hiring-advice/intervi (accessed November 19, 2017).

4. Why did you leave your last position?

5. Tell me why you applied for this position?

6. Why do you want to work for us?

7. What are your career goals? Three years from now? Five years from now?

8. Why should I hire you?

9. What are your salary expectations?

10. Do you have any questions for me?

20 interview questions that you should not ask and their "legal" alternatives.

Common sense tells us that we can't ask questions about marriage, children, illegal activity (that's what a background check is for), religious or political affiliation, credit history, or social affiliations. However, there are many cases where simply rewording a question can make it askable. We've rewritten 20 interview questions that you can ask without getting into trouble for discrimination.

Nationality

1. "ARE YOU A U.S. CITIZEN?"

While this may seem like a seemingly straightforward question to decide workplace eligibility, it is strictly hands-off. Instead of asking about citizenship, pose the question in a light that is reflective of authorization to work period.

INSTEAD, ASK: "ARE YOU AUTHORIZED TO WORK IN THE U.S.?"

2. "HOW LONG HAVE YOU LIVED HERE?"

Familiarity with a city or town may be important to the job that which you are hiring. However, it is important not to ask an interviewee about their residency. Instead, try asking directly about their current situation. They can always volunteer more information later.

INSTEAD ASK: "WHAT IS YOUR CURRENT ADDRESS? DO YOU HAVE ANY ALTERNATIVE LOCATIONS WHERE YOU CAN BE REACHED?"

Religion

3. "WHAT RELIGION DO YOU PRACTICE?"

You may want to find out about an interviewees religion to determine their weekend availability, but it is important you do not ask this question. Alternatively, directly ask about their availability to work on the weekends.[5]

INSTEAD, ASK: "WHAT DAYS ARE YOU AVAILABLE TO WORK?"

4. "DO YOU BELONG TO A CLUB OR SOCIAL ORGANIZATION?"

This particular question could be too revealing of political or religious affiliation or activity. Also, this question has little or no relevance to a job candidate's abilities or qualifications. However, if you want to ask this question, it is important to focus the wording on work.

INSTEAD, ASK: "ARE YOU A MEMBER OF A PROFESSIONAL OR TRADE GROUP THAT IS RELEVANT TO OUR INDUSTRY?"

Age

5. "HOW OLD ARE YOU?"

While this may seem like a seemingly harmless question, it is quite loaded. Asking about an interviewee's age can ultimately set you up for discrimination based on age. Just to be safe, you can make sure they are old enough to work for you.

5   10 Interview Questions You Can't Ask And 10 Legal .., http://www.getpayroll.com/payroll-academy /2017/5/11/10-interview-questions-you-c (accessed November 19, 2017).

INSTEAD, ASK: "ARE YOU OVER THE AGE OF 18?"

6. "HOW MUCH LONGER DO YOU PLAN TO WORK BEFORE YOU RETIRE?"

Once again, this type of question leaves you vulnerable to discrimination allegations later on down the road. While you may not want to hire someone who is planning on retiring in a few years, you can not dismiss an interviewee for these reasons alone. Instead, ask about the candidate's future career goals.

INSTEAD, ASK: "WHAT ARE YOUR LONG-TERM CAREER GOALS?"

Marital and Family Status

7. "DO YOU PLAN TO HAVE CHILDREN?"

It is clear that with this question the concern is any family obligations that may interfere with work hours. Instead of making it personal and asking about family issues, get straight to the point of work schedules and availability.[6]

INSTEAD ASK: "ARE YOU AVAILABLE TO WORK OVERTIME ON OCCASION? CAN YOU TRAVEL?"

8. "WHO IS YOUR CLOSEST RELATIVE TO NOTIFY IN CASE OF AN EMERGENCY?"

Although this question is not completely off-putting, you are assuming the interviewee's personal life. They could very easily not be close with any of their family members.

INSTEAD, ASK: "IN THE CASE OF AN EMERGENCY, WHO SHOULD WE NOTIFY?"

9. "DO YOU HAVE KIDS?"

This particular question is for people who may be working with children. The fact that they may have additional experience with children at home may be a bonus for you. However, refrain from asking this question. Instead, ask about the interviewee's experience, and they may volunteer additional information that way.

INSTEAD, ASK: "WHAT IS YOUR EXPERIENCE WITH "X" AGE GROUP?"

6   10 Interview Questions You Can't Ask And 10 Legal .., http://www.getpayroll.com/payroll-academy
/2017/5/11/10-interview-questions-you-c (accessed November 20, 2017).

10. "WHAT DO YOUR PARENTS DO FOR A LIVING?"

Asking an interviewee about their parents can reveal a lot. However, this job is not directly related to their ability to do this job. However, if you are trying to find out if your interviewee's family has worked in your industry before, this question is a good way to find out.

INSTEAD ASK: "TELL ME HOW YOU BECAME INTERESTED IN THE "X" INDUSTRY."

11. "IF YOU GET PREGNANT, WILL YOU CONTINUE TO WORK, AND WILL YOU COME BACK AFTER MATERNITY LEAVE?"

Ultimately, you want to be able to invest your time into a candidate that will end up sticking around, but you can't ask a woman to share her pregnancy plans, or lack thereof, with you.[7]

INSTEAD, ASK: "WHAT ARE YOUR LONG-TERM CAREER GOALS?"

Gender

12. "HOW DO YOU FEEL ABOUT SUPERVISING MEN/WOMEN?"

This question, although it may seem like a valid concern, is not acceptable. The candidate may not have any issues working with the opposite or same sex, and you'll seem crass for even bringing it up.

INSTEAD, ASK: "TELL ME ABOUT YOUR PREVIOUS EXPERIENCE MANAGING TEAMS."

13. "WHAT DO YOU THINK OF INTEROFFICE DATING?"

Interoffice dating can be distracting, could potentially break up teams and cause a whole number of other problems in the workplace. However, asking this particular question makes assumptions about the candidates marital status and could also be perceived as a come-on.

INSTEAD, ASK: "HAVE YOU EVER BEEN DISCIPLINED FOR YOUR BEHAVIOR AT WORK?"

---

7   10 More Interview Questions You Can't Ask And 10 Legal .., http://www.getpayroll.com/payroll-academy /2017/7/14/10-more-interview-questions- (accessed November 20, 2017).

Health and Physical Abilities

14."DO YOU SMOKE OR DRINK?"

As an employer, you would want to avoid a potential candidate that has a drinking problem or will take multiple smoke breaks throughout the workday. It can also be a potential insurance concern. Instead of directly asking about this, find out if they have had some trouble with health policies in the past.

INSTEAD, ASK: "IN THE PAST, HAVE YOU BEEN DISCIPLINED FOR VIOLATING COMPANY POLICIES FORBIDDING THE USE OF ALCOHOL OR TOBACCO PRODUCTS?"

15."DO YOU TAKE DRUGS?"

This particular question is just a misunderstanding of terms. Your potential candidate may think you are asking them about prescription drugs, which is off-limits. Make sure you are specific about illegal substances instead of legal prescription ones.[8]

INSTEAD, ASK: "DO YOU USE ILLEGAL DRUGS?"

16."HOW MUCH DO YOU WEIGH?"

Asking about someone's weight is incredibly personal and is often an embarrassing for most individuals. Most of the time it is also not necessarily relevant to a candidates ability to do even a physical labor job. Avoid making assumptions, and ask about abilities directly.

INSTEAD, ASK: "ARE YOU ABLE TO LIFT BOXES WEIGHING UP TO 50 POUNDS?"

Miscellaneous Questions

17."DO YOU HAVE ANY DISABILITIES?"

Disabilities, whether they're physical or mental, may affect a candidate's ability to do the job assigned, but it is very important, critical even, that you avoid asking about them. Instead, find out if the applicant can handle doing what is required of the job description.

INSTEAD, ASK: "ARE YOU ABLE TO PERFORM THE SPECIFIC DUTIES OF THIS POSITION?"

8 10 More Interview Questions You Can't Ask And 10 Legal .., http://www.getpayroll.com/payroll-academy
/2017/7/14/10-more-interview-questions- (accessed November 20, 2017).

18."HOW FAR IS YOUR COMMUTE?"

Although hiring an employee who lives close by may be convenient, you cannot choose candidates based on their location. Instead, find out about their availability.

INSTEAD, ASK: "ARE YOU ABLE TO WORK AT 8 A.M.?"

19."HAVE YOU EVER BEEN ARRESTED?"

In sensitive positions, like ones in which people are dealing with money, you may want to find out about your candidate's legal background. But ensure that you ask only directly about crimes that relate to your concerns.[9]

INSTEAD, ASK: "HAVE YOU EVER BEEN CONVICTED OF "X" (FRAUD, THEFT, ETC.)

20."WERE YOU HONORABLY DISCHARGED FROM THE MILITARY?"

A bad military record can be rather illuminating. However, you cannot ask about it. Instead, ask about the candidate's experience in the military. They may volunteer this information on their own.[10]

INSTEAD, ASK: "TELL ME HOW YOUR EXPERIENCE IN THE MILITARY CAN BENEFIT OUR COMPANY."

One last interviewing tip.

Many interviewers take a cavalier attitude towards interviewing. After all, they'll never see them again if they weren't hired. You never know how a candidate will feel after leaving the interview and what actions they may or may not take as a result of how they felt they were treated during the interview. Ask the right questions, document their answers, and be consistent in each interview.

Finally, **do not interview alone.** If possible, have another person interview with you. That way, there will never be an opportunity for a he-said-she-said situation if you are ever charged with discrimination.

9   10 More Interview Questions You Can't Ask And 10 Legal .., http://www.getpayroll.com/payroll-academy /2017/7/14/10-more-interview-questions- (accessed November 20, 2017).

10 10 More Interview Questions You Can't Ask And 10 Legal .., http://www.getpayroll.com/payroll-academy /2017/7/14/10-more-interview-questions- (accessed November 21, 2017).

What's a PEO and how can it affect me?

S mall business owners have limited budgets and limited time. You need help with business management tasks such as payroll, employee benefits, and human resources but can't afford an assistant. This is where a PEO comes in.

What is a PEO and how does it work?

According to Wikipedia, "A **professional employer organization** (PEO) is a firm that provides a service under which an employer can outsource employee management tasks, such as employee benefits, payroll and workers' compensation, recruiting, risk/safety management, and training and development. The PEO does this by hiring a client company's employees, thus becoming their employer of record for tax purposes and insurance purposes. This practice is known as co-employment."

(Source: https://en.wikipedia.org/wiki/Professional_employer_organization)

A PEO enters into a joint-employment relationship or co-employment, with a business owner by leasing employees to the employer (owner), thereby allowing the PEO to share and manage many employer-related responsibilities and liabilities.

PEOs typically serve as a professional employer of their clients' employees. The client company reports its wages under the PEO's federal employer identification number (FEIN), and employee liability shifts to the PEO. Employers gain economies of scale by having more benefits options, sometimes at lower rates, and in some cases can use the PEO's state unemployment tax and workers' compensation rates, which may also be lower than the employer's rate.

Depending on the PEO and the contract, a few or all of the human resources functions can be outsourced. An administrative services outsourcing (ASO) agreement provides options for companies that are not interested in co-employment but want some of the outsourcing benefits.

How PEO's began.

PEO's began in the 1960's as a way to escape Federal ERISA requirements. If you had no employees, you were exempt from ERISA. The Federal Government has long since repapered those rules.

PEOs have been used to reduce workers compensation costs to their clients. Several PEO leaders have gone to jail for improperly reporting workers compensation risks and thereby illegally reducing the premiums they were being charged.

PEOs were front and center in the State Unemployment dumping scandals to improperly reduce State Unemployment taxes for a company. It all stopped when George Bush signed the anti-dumping law in 2004, and most States adopted similar rules.

Advantages to signing up with a PEO.

The purpose of a PEO is to allow a business not to have to spend time on certain functions and concentrate on other areas.

There can be significant advantages of a PEO, especially for a small employer that may not have the much experience with human resources. The burdens a PEO can relieve from human resources are the following:

Benefits administration.

Typically, with PEO-sponsored benefit plans, your employees will have access to a wider variety of benefits that your company could obtain on its own. Benefits include medical, dental and vision coverage, a health care flexible spending account, a retirement plan, life insurance and personal accident insurance, short-term and long-term disability insurance, adoption assistance, commuter benefits and educational assistance.[1]

---

1   What Is A Peo? | Learn What To Expect From A Peo, https://www.insperity.com/blog/what-is-a-peo/ (accessed November 21, 2017).

Recruiting and hiring.

A PEO can help you design the ideal recruitment process that fits your unique business. It may also work with you to develop job descriptions, conduct wage, and salary surveys, and improve your hiring managers' interview and candidate selection skills.

PEO helps you manage your liabilities as an employer, providing employee handbooks, new hire onboarding, termination assistance, leave of absence request management, employee relations support, drug testing services, liability management training, employment verification, and more.

Payroll administration.

The PEO processes payroll for your employees, including managing the regular compensation of your employees, along with payroll record maintenance and management, payroll compliance, online paystubs and W-2s, payroll management reports, garnishment and deduction administration and PTO accruals.[2]

Workers' compensation administration.

Joining a PEO provides you with workers' compensation insurance coverage. The PEO also manages and resolves an injured employee claims in the event of an on-site injury. To prevent injuries before they even happen, PEOs offer workplace loss prevention reviews. Its loss prevention specialists can work with your company to design loss prevention and return-to-work programs.[3]

Sounds pretty great, right? Well, not so fast.

A PEO is supposed to relieve a business owner of the burden of administering critical employee-related functions, reduce liabilities, increase competitiveness, and improve the bottom line of their customers. **Is that really the case?**

The reality of a PEO agreement.

What PEO's really do is provide a way for employers to buy insurance products, payroll processing, and possibly some

basic human resources services in a single package **with a high administrative cost added on top**.

PEO policies state that they, "Assume certain employer rights, responsibilities, and risk." Therein lies the issue.

---

2 Ibid.

3 What Is A Peo? | Learn What To Expect From A Peo, https://www.insperity.com/blog/what-is-a-peo/ (accessed November 21, 2017).

Many of the States in which they operate disagree. **Most States have rules that PEO's are co-employers or joint employers and that the actual employer retains all of the risks.** Unfortunately, PEO companies do not share that part in their marketing materials.

Disadvantages of a PEO

There are many disadvantages of using a PEO, and reasons why companies abandon them.

1. **The loss of control of essential processes and people.**

   - Under a PEO, a business owner gives up the control for choosing the vendors that which he wants to work.

2. **Security issues with the vendor's system.**

   - If the PEO selects a bad vendor, the business owner suffers the consequences.

3. **Viewed differently by the IRS and insurance carriers.**

   - Your business is no longer considered a unique entity and cannot establish workers comp experience and unemployment ratings of its own. *(source:* https://www.peocompare.com/PEO-disadvantages-5-reasons-companies-abandon-them/*)*

4. **An outside company's influence on your culture, processes, and policies.**

   a. The PEO will have a strict policy that you must follow for hiring, training, disciplining and firing. You are forced to be compliant with their rules.

   b. Your diminished value as an internal HR professional.

   c. Lack of control and security over employee paperwork.

5. **Resistance from employees.**

- The lack of objectivity that an owner provides and a PEO that can affect morale problems if all employees are not treated fairly and the same.

6. **Your independent contractors need to stay as 1099s.**

- There simply would be no benefit for using a PEO as the services they offer have no impact on a 1099 contractor.

7. **Monetary risk.**

- Many PEOs require you pay for their services upfront before work begins. If the PEO is sold or goes out of business, you could be stuck or out of luck.

8. **Loss of perceived value.**

- The average PEO costs between $800 to well over $1,000 per employee each year. Those numbers quickly add up with each employee and are fees and profits you have no need to pay.

The Facts of a PEO- What's in it and what are you paying?

What it comes down to is this: A PEO says it will use a large number of employees it has to negotiate better rates for medical insurance policies that small businesses can themselves. If you are the small business, you have to take the policy that the PEO has negotiated.

Since high benefit policies are easier to negotiate, small businesses will (many times) find they are **buying a Cadillac health insurance policy when they want to buy a Ford**. The Cadillac policy is cheaper than what the small business could buy it for, but it is still way more expensive than the Ford policy they could have negotiated on their own. What Obamacare and State Exchanges are going to do to the PEO insurance field is still way up in the air.

The PEO will do the same thing with Workers Compensation Insurance. They will bundle up a whole bunch of risks and try to get a better rate from the insurance company. They may also maintain a staff whose sole purpose is to minimize payouts of workers compensation claims to your employees. **Those payouts affect the PEO's experience rating and drive up their costs**. When your employees don't get compensation for their injuries like they think they should, are they going to blame the PEO or you, their employer?

Over the years, PEO's have attracted the worst risks because those risks received the greatest benefit from a better workers compensation rate from the PEO. This, of course, was a self-defeating proposition for the PEO. Those bad risks drove up the premium cost to the PEO with no benefit to the PEO.

In the current environment, many States and many workers compensation carriers require individual underwriting of each client company of the PEO. Since the underwriting is just the small businessman's company and the experience rating is just accidents involving his employees and since the State sets rates; the advantage of being in a PEO employment pool is gone. It is an extra charge for the PEO administering your workers compensation, which administration for many companies is worth little or nothing.

To be or not to be HR services?

Many of the PEOs brag about their Human Resource departments and what they bring to your business. For many small businesses that is little or nothing. Why?

They don't actually hire people for you.

They don't actually fire people for you.

When an employee has a complaint, the PEO is off in some other City or State.

When an employee has a personal problem and needs a shoulder to cry on, it is still the small business owner's shoulder that gets cried on.

If the PEO supplies the employee handbook, you are stuck with it. If they don't supply an employee handbook, you still have to create your own.

Since most small businesses don't have heavy HR requirements a heavily staffed HR department is a cost that the small business owner neither needs nor wants. If your employees are in a much larger pool that a PEO requires, it makes them subject to more, not less, Federal and State regulations. Those regulations cost time and money to oversee and report; costs you are assuming. If the employee were just your employee, they and you would not be subject to the regulations at all.

PEO and FMLA

The Family and Medical Leave Act (FMLA) gives employees that are eligible coverage for unpaid, job-protected leave for family and medical reasons. Employers with 50 employers or more are covered by FMLA.

How does that translate when working with a PEO?

According to the U.S. Department of Labor Wage and Hour Division, when a company works with a PEO they become joint employers. "Joint employment exists when an employee is employed by two (or more) employers such that the employers are responsible for compliance with the FMLA."[4] Joint employment determines employ-

4   Fact Sheet #28n: Joint Employment And Primary And .., https://www.dol.gov/whd/regs/compliance/whdfs28n.pdf (accessed November 21, 2017).

ee coverage under the FMLA, and responsibilities vary depending on who is the primary and secondary employers of the employee who is taking leave.

When an individual is employed by two employers in a joint employment relationship under the FMLA, in most cases one employer will be the primary employer while the other will be the secondary employer. Determining whether an employer is a primary or secondary employer depends upon the particular facts of the situation. Factors to consider include:

- who has authority to hire and fire, and to place or assign work to the employee;

- who decides how, when, and the amount that the employee is paid; and,

- who provides the employee's leave or other employment benefits.

In the case of a temporary placement or staffing agency, the agency is most commonly the primary employer.[5]

The business owner is most likely going to be the secondary employer. That means you are prohibited from interfering with the employees FMLA rights. You also cannot fire or discriminate against an employee for "opposing a practice that is unlawful under the FMLA." In some States, you may also find yourself with paid Family Leave and all of the costs and disruptions to your business that will be imposed because of the PEO, and not because of your own operation.

PEO and payroll processing. Are there risks?

PEOs do pay the payroll taxes and file the quarterly and annual forms **as the employer of record.** What if the PEO goes out of business? Is the IRS is going to write off any unpaid taxes?

The *small businessman will find that the IRS deems them a "Responsible Party" and they will be forced to pay the taxes the PEO did not, even if they already paid the payroll taxes to the PEO company.*

PEO Payroll Billing

Typically, a PEO will add their fees to your costs:

They calculate their costs, *plus*

Add on an administrative fee, *plus*

Add on a profit margin, *and*

Add the total as a percentage of your payroll costs.

5   Fact Sheet #28n: Joint Employment And Primary And .., https://www.dol.gov/whd/regs/compliance/whdfs28n.pdf (accessed November 22, 2017).

Each pay period you turn in your hours and salaries to the PEO company. The PEO representative tells you what you have to wire them their fees so they can process the payroll. The **administrative fee can run from 4% of the real costs too much higher**. The PEO will normally be very reluctant to discuss their actual costs so that you can see that which you are paying.

Our experience has shown...

Our experience with PEO's goes way back to when they were still called staff leasing. We've discovered that PEO's try to make their bills absolutely impenetrable, and **we are CPA's and experts at deciphering this financial jargon**. They also neglect to lower your cost as your employees max out for SUTA, FUTA, and even FICA.

If you are a small business, it's cheaper to negotiate your own insurance.

Our experience over the last 20 years is that it is never cheaper to use a PEO. If you negotiate your own medical and workers compensation insurance, have a good online HR service when needed, and use a good payroll processing service bureau with CPAs on staff - **you, will save money.**

Your savings should be at least $1,000.00 per employee per year and sometimes more than twice that.

One of our best customers, owned by doctors with 150 or so employees, was talked into looking at a PEO a few years ago. The business manager was a very sharp person and had minimized costs for years. The PEO quote was $300,000.00 per year *higher* for the same services that the business was getting. The doctor changed his mind.

Before going with a PEO analyze what they are offering you and what it is worth to you.

With the SHOP exchanges and the rest of the Affordable Care Act, a one-stop- shop is going to be very enticing. But if you have 20 employees you may be taking a $50,000 hit to your bottom line and getting little or nothing out of it.

Talk to a payroll company with CPAs on staff.

They should be able to bring in one or more independent insurance agents and one or more online HR services. GetPayroll does that for our clients.

PEO versus a payroll provider. What's the difference?

PEOs are co-employers, meaning that they share the employer's responsibilities.

When a company enters into a contract with a PEO, its employees become employees of the PEO. This allows the PEO to pool the employees of many smaller companies together to get better rates on health insurance, workers' compensation, and state unemployment. Many also offer HR services, which allow the businesses to outsource the HR management function. Also, PEOs are typically regulated at the state level.[6]

Payroll providers, on the other hand, are not co-employers.

While they process payroll and file taxes on a client's behalf, the client's employees do not become the provider's employees. Many providers offer HR software, but, unlike PEOs, the HR function remains in-house. The key difference is that these tools help in-house employees become more efficient.[7]

An easy HR alternative is a click away.

At GetPayroll, we have come across numerous businesses offering HR services to small business. Give us a call at 972-353-0000, and we recommend one that has flexible package options to help grow your business and strengthen your HR offerings.

Compare GetPayroll and Simon Payroll App to a PEO.

Are you with a **PEO?**
Don't Get Robbed! Compare GetPayroll & Simon to Your PEO.

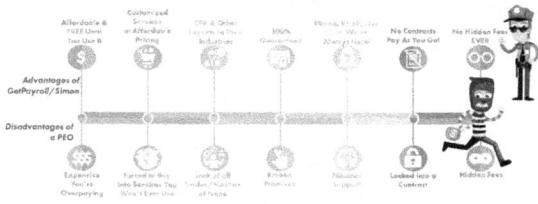

At GetPayroll & Simon, we normally save clients $1,000 on EACH employee EVERY year. We have a program with partners to provide all the services a PEO offers as a complete package, including payroll, insurance, benefits, human resources and more!
www.getpayroll.com. 972-353-0000.

GetPayroll
Simon

---

6 Pros And Cons Of Using Peo Companies | Paycor | Paycor, https://www.paycor.com/resource-center/pros-and-cons-of-using-a-peo (accessed November 22, 2017).

7 Pros And Cons Of Using Peo Companies | Paycor | Paycor, https://www.paycor.com/resource-center/pros-and-cons-of-using-a-peo (accessed November 22, 2017).

Mean Tweets: True stories from salon and spa business owners.

#thestruggleisreal

Before we leave you, we want to share our "Mean Tweets: True Stories from Small Business Owners" and particular tweets come from salon and spa owners. We hope you get a good laugh over them and feel for them at the same time.

The next time something happens at work that you sit back and say, "What the? Why is this happening to me? Am I the only one?" Now you know, you're not. Enjoy.

Mean Tweets: True Stories from Salon and Spa Small Business Owners

"A spa competitor used to make phantom appointments on my book to fill it with bogus appointments. #competitionisab*t#h"

"The salon down the street copied all my brand colors, my website, and then tried to hire my employees out from under me. She then started saying she bought my businesses and will be merging locations soon. Yea, you heard me right."

"How do you tell your employee that they need to bathe more than 3x a week?! #thatsmellisntsweet #beprofessional"

Watch Our Mean Tweets Part 1!

http://bit.ly/GPtweet1

A spa competitor used to make phantom appointments on my books to fill it with bogus appointments. #competitionisabitch

"My employee asked me why he has to pay Mississippi tax when he works in Texas? I said because you live in Mississippi" #How ManyTimesDoIHaveToExpalinThis

"I just love when you work in the beauty business, and your employee comes waltzing in with greasy hair and no makeup."

"My employee quit in a hellfire and then called the police saying I wouldn't return her personal possessions that she left behind. What did I have to give the police when they arrived? Her coffee mug. Imagine the cops expression."

Watch Our Mean Tweets Part 2!

http://bit.ly/GPtweet2

My Employee quit in hellfire and then called the police saying I wouldn't return her personal possessions that she left behind. Wha

"NO! I will not make you a 1099 contractor, so you don't have to pay child support."

"I love it when an employee starts blabbing about how much money I must have because he knows how much he brings in."

"I got a text from my receptionist on Friday morning quitting his job. On Monday he called and asked for his job back. WTH?"

Watch Our Mean Tweets Part 3!

http://bit.ly/GPtweet3

NO! I will not make you a 1099 contractor so you don't have to pay child support.

"it didn't take long after I fired one of my sales reps for him to start contacting my customers and informing them that we were closing our doors and that they shouldn't bother paying their invoices."[1] #damagecontrol

"The State said I have to pay one of my employees unemployment even though I fired her because I caught her stealing and decided to be nice and not have her arrested." #getthehelloutofhere

"I walked into the office this morning and I asked one of my employees what was on his agenda today. His response was "Don't know. I didn't come here to work today."

1 Firing Horror Stories - Spread Lies (7) - Cnnmoney, http://money.cnn.com/galleries/2011/smallbusiness/1108/gallery.firing_horror_sto (accessed November 22, 2017).

Watch Our Mean Tweets Part 4!

http://bit.ly/GPtweet4

"Joe is out "sick," if sick means out at the beach all day. Did he forget we are friends on Facebook?

"I caught one of my employees sleeping at her desk. She told me she was "reaching for her pencil." For 7 minutes............ #sooveremployees

"A web developer we fired a few years ago recently completed a 90-day prison sentence for hacking into our servers."

Watch our Mean Tweets Part 5!

http://bit.ly/GPtweet5

Joe is out "sick", if sick means out at the beach all day.
Did he forget we are friends on Facebook?

"My staff started complaining when I told them I would no longer allow clients to tip on the credit card. Even though I explained how I was charged a fee for their tip. I offered to continue and take it out of their pay. Oh No! That's Not Fair...blah blah blah."

"I had a stylist quit through a text message and then try to collect unemployment. I got a good laugh out of that one."

"Two of my ex-employees got together and decided to open a business .01 miles outside of my 10-mile radius non-compete zone and then sent letters to all of my clients that they stole contact information for."

Watch our Mean Tweets Part 6!

http://bit.ly/GPtweet6

My staff started

"Employees are great mathematicians when their check is short a penny. Ooooh but if they are double paid, they suddenly become clueless."

"I caught one of my massage therapists putting her personal flyers in the coffee shop next to my spa. When I confronted her she was like "what?" all stupid and such. What was she thinking?"

"I caught one of my estheticians heating up her bagel sandwich in the hot towel cabby. Eweeeeeee."

Watch our Mean Tweets Part 7!

http://bit.ly/GPtweet7

"My employee came up to me yesterday and said, "Who's FICA and why are they getting 7% of my check?""

"I have a hairstylist who usually looks great but has come in a few times wearing this crazy purple wig that looks ridiculous. Now I have to tell her to stop. Why me!"

"I had a stylist contact the labor board and file a discrimination suit against me for firing her for poor performance. WTF? #bringiton"

Watch our Mean Tweets Part 8!

http://bit.ly/GPtweet8

I have a hairstylist who usually looks great but has come in a

"I had a client come in late for her massage appointment. When she came out to the front desk to pay, she got out her calculator to deduct the number of minutes she missed from her appointment. Um, I don't think so."

"I am a relatively new salon and have only been opened since September, and already 3 staff members have walked out I am really struggling to find self-employed people who are committed to actually working! Ugh!"

"My employee fussed because she said she was underpaid. She brought her bank statement to me to prove that she was underpaid only to realize she had $200 in bank fees deduced in overdraft charges."

Watch our Mean Tweets Part 9!

http://bit.ly/GPtweet9

I had a client come in late for her massage appointment. When she came out to the front desk to pay, she got out her calculator to deduct the amount of minutes she missed from her appointment. Um, I don't think so. #tryagain #uhno

"Brenda had her mother call me to say she wouldn't be at work today. Brenda is 49."

"Do I really have to report my tips. No! Only the IRS insists!"

"My employee came into my office stating that she wanted a cost of living raise of 4%. I told her that cost of doing business went up 6% so I'll need cut her pay by 2%. #mouthdroppedtothefloor"

Watch our Mean Tweets Part 10!

http://bit.ly/GPtweet10

"Brenda

"I hired a new esthetician, and she asked if she could bring in a new product line to use in her treatment room and to retail. I said yes and spent over $1200. She quit 3 weeks later."

"I hired a "licensed" massage therapist only to find out her license was a fake. Did she really think I wouldn't check?"

"I accidentally double paid my entire staff! While most came forward and were honest, 3 were not and quickly spent their money. They now want a payment plan to pay me back what they owe me. Um, no."

Watch our Mean Tweets Part 11!

http://bit.ly/GPtweet11

I hired a "licensed" massage therapist only to find out her license
was a fake. Did she really think I wouldn't check? #whatthewhat #s

"I hired a massage therapist, and when I wasn't looking, they placed their own personal business cards out on the table in the treatment room to steal clients from my business. Needless to say, my client told me, and they were fired immediately."

Bob showed up for work after being a no-show for 2 weeks, and he wonders why his stuff is packed up."

"How do you get stuck in traffic when you live close enough to walk to work?!"

Watch our Mean Tweets Part 12!

http://bit.ly/GPtweet12

How do you get stuck in traffic when you live close enough to walk to work?!
#thinkofanotherexcuse #weknowtherealstory #areyouserious

We truly get it. #thestruggleisreal

Follow our YouTube channel

Get notified of new Mean Tweet videos.

https://www.youtube.com/channel/UCxs-_RwC9NgfUcqbwvEaMIQ?view_as=sub-scriber

Bibliography

5 Interviewing Mistakes Hiring Managers Should Avoid .., https://hiring.monster.
com/hr/hr-best-practices/recruiting-hiring-advice/intervi (accessed November
19, 2017).

Ibid.

7 Reasons You Still Need Business Cards - The Balance, https://www.thebalance.
com/why-use-business-cards-2947920 (accessed November 18, 2017).

10 Interview Questions You Can't Ask And 10 Legal .., http://www.getpayroll.com/
payroll-academy/2017/5/11/10-interview-questions-you-c (accessed November 19, 2017).

Ibid., (accessed November 20, 2017).

14 Highly Effective Ways To Motivate Employees | Inc.com, https://www.inc.com/
ilya-pozin/14-highly-effective-ways-to-motivate-employees.ht (accessed
November 11, 2017).

Ibid

Acceptable Reasons For Termination - The Hartford, https://www.thehartford.com/
business-playbook/in-depth/valid-reasons-fire-employ (accessed November 8,
2017).

Ibid.

Accounting Setup For Startups - Slideshare, https://www.slideshare.net/Incuba8/
accounting-setup-for-startups (accessed November 6, 2017).

Accounting Setup For Startups, Slidesearchengine.com, http://www.slidesearch-
engine.com/slide/accounting-setup-for-startups/plus (accessed November 5,
2017)

Accounting Setup For Startups - Slideshare, https://www.slideshare.net/Incuba8/
accounting-setup-for-startups (accessed November 5, 2017).

Accounting Setup For Startups, Slidesearchengine.com, http://www.slidesearch-
engine.com/slide/accounting-setup-for-startups/plus (accessed November 23,
2017).

Bringing On New Employees? Don't Let Applications .., http://www.hrhero.com/hl/
articles/2017/09/29/bringing-on-new-employees-dont-let- (accessed November 19, 2017).

Clark, Kent, and Cathy Jensen. 2015. "What to Expect When the IRS Audits Your Community." PM. Public Management 97 (4). International City/County Management Association: 16.

Compliance Connection | Federal Tax Calculations, https://adp-iat.adp.com/tools-and-resources/compliance-connection/federal-taxes/ (accessed November 4, 2017).

Definition Of Marketing, https://www.ama.org/AboutAMA/Pages/Definition-of-Marketing.aspx (accessed November 18, 2017).

Depositing Federal Income, Social Security & Medicare Taxes, http://www.rlsire.com/FAQ/FrequentlyAskedQuestions_files/content/Fed_deposit.htm (accessed November 9, 2017).

Elaws - Employment Laws Assistance For Workers And Small .., https://webapps.dol.gov/elaws/whd/flsa/docs/volunteers.asp (accessed November 7, 2017).

Encouraging Your Employees To Lead | The Trocchio Advantage, https://trocchio-advantage.com/encouraging-your-employees-to-lead/ (accessed November 13, 2017).

Ibid.

Fact Sheet #28n: Joint Employment And Primary And .., https://www.dol.gov/whd/regs/compliance/whdfs28n.pdf (accessed November 21, 2017).

Fact Sheet #28n: Joint Employment And Primary And .., https://www.dol.gov/whd/regs/compliance/whdfs28n.pdf (accessed November 22, 2017).

Family And Medical Leave Act - Wage And Hour Division (whd .., https://www.dol.gov/whd/fmla/index.htm (accessed November 14, 2017).

Fashion Marketing Flashcards | Quizlet, https://quizlet.com/185001096/fashion-marketing-flash-cards/ (accessed November 18, 2017).

Firing Horror Stories - Spread Lies (7) - Cnnmoney, http://money.cnn.com/galleries/2011/smallbusiness/1108/gallery.firing_horror_sto (accessed November 22, 2017).

Forms 941 And 944 – Deposit Requirements, https://taxmap.irs.gov/taxmap/taxtp/Tt750_16-007.htm (accessed November 4, 2017).

Ibid.

How And When To Make Payroll Tax Deposits, https://www.thebalance.com/how-and-when-do-i-make-payroll-tax-deposits-398821 (accessed November 16, 2017).

How To Process Payroll And Payroll Taxes - The Balance, https://www.thebalance.com/how-do-i-process-payroll-and-payroll-taxes-398711 (accessed November 16, 2017).

How To Set Up A Yearly Payroll Tax Calendar - The Balance, https://www.thebalance.com/how-to-set-up-a-yearly-payroll-tax-calendar-397319 (accessed November 17, 2017).

How To Set Up A Yearly Payroll Tax Calendar - The Balance, https://www.thebalance.com/how-to-set-up-a-yearly-payroll-tax-calendar-397319 (accessed November 17, 2017).

How To Set Up A Yearly Payroll Tax Calendar - The Balance, https://www.thebalance.com/how-to-set-up-a-yearly-payroll-tax-calendar-397319 (accessed November 18, 2017).

Independent Contractor Agreement 1 - Anyform.org, http://anyform.org/doc/14563/independent-contractor-agreement-1 (accessed November 7, 2017).

Ibid.

Independent Contractor Agreement 1 - Anyform.org, http://anyform.org/doc/14563/independent-contractor-agreement-1 (accessed November 8, 2017).

Independent Contractor Agreement - Chapman University, https://www.chapman.edu/research/institutes-and-centers/leatherby-center/_files/ (accessed November 7, 2017).

Ibid.

Independent Contractor Agreement - Tidyform, https://www.tidyform.com/download/file/independent-contractor-agreement-1/pdf (accessed November 7, 2017).

Ibid.

Independent Contractor Agreement - Tidyform, https://www.tidyform.com/download/file/independent-contractor-agreement-1/pdf (accessed November 8, 2017).

Independent Contractor Self Employed Or Employee .., https://www.irs.gov/businesses/small-businesses-self-employed/independent-contra (accessed November 6, 2017).

Irs 20 Questions W2 Vs 1099 - Home | Gala Choruses, http://galachoruses.org/sites/default/files/IRS-20-questions-W2-vs-1099.pdf (accessed November 4, 2017).

January 16, 2002 Memorandum, http://www.ncpublicschools.org/docs/fbs/resources/memos/withholdingrequirements. (accessed November 5, 2017).

Knowing What Makes Your Employees Tick, https://www.predictiveindex.com/blog/knowing-what-makes-your-employees-tick/ (accessed November 12, 2017).

Luxe Salon And Spa Manual, http://luxesalonaz.com/wp-content/uploads/2012/03/Luxe-Salon-and-Spa-Manual.pdf (accessed November 15, 2017).

Milestones: 1977 - Equal Employment Opportunity Commission, https://www.eeoc.gov/eeoc/history/50th/milestones/1977.cfm?renderforprint=1 (accessed November 8, 2017).

Most Popular Business Terms Flashcards | Quizlet, https://quizlet.com/62158835/most-popular-business-terms-flash-cards/ (accessed November 18, 2017).

Need To Know What Belongs In An Employee Handbook?, https://www.thebalance.com/need-to-know-what-goes-in-an-employee-handbook-191830 (accessed November 15, 2017).

Part 1- Independent Contractor Vs. An Employee .., http://www.getpayroll.com/payroll-academy/pa170801 (accessed November 3, 2017).

Ibid.

Ibid., (accessed November 25, 2017).

Payroll Taxes - Jkkr.com, http://www.jkkr.com/content/client/2a738ed4da-c6a6818a3222c7d150bcde/uploads/5-bu (accessed November 5, 2017).

Ibid., (accessed November 6, 2017).

Payroll Tax Penalties, When The Irs Sends A Letter. - Www .., https://www.ralphcoutard.com/payroll-tax-penalties-when-the-irs-sends-a-letter/ (accessed November 9, 2017).

Ibid., (accessed November 9, 2017).

Ibid.

Publication 15 - Circular E, Employer's Tax Guide - 11 .., https://taxmap.irs.gov/tax-map/archive2012/taxmap/pubs/p15-010.htm (accessed November 10, 2017).

Ibid., (accessed November 16, 2017).

Ibid.

Sample Employee Handbook For Web - Northeast - Niqca, http://www.niqca.org/documents/Employee_Handbook.pdf (accessed November 15, 2017).

Statutory Nonemployees | Internal Revenue Service, https://www.irs.gov/businesses/small-businesses-self-employed/statutory-nonemplo (accessed November 3, 2017).

Selected Supreme Court Decisions - Eeoc ... - Eeoc Home Page, https://www.eeoc.gov/eeoc/history/35th/thelaw/supreme_court.html (accessed November 8, 2017).

Ibid.

Taos Business Kit, Payroll Taxes - Taoscpa.com, http://www.taoscpa.com/payroll_taxes.html (accessed November 4, 2017).

Tax Withholding For Government Workers | Internal Revenue .., https://www.irs.gov/government-entities/federal-state-local-governments/tax-with (accessed November 3, 2017).

The Irs 20 Point List For Classifying Employees | Primepay, https://primepay.com/blog/irs-20-point-list-classifying-employees (accessed November 3, 2017).

The Ripple Effects You Create As A Manager, https://hbr.org/2013/05/the-ripple-effects-you-create (accessed November 11, 2017).

Ibid., (accessed November 12, 2017).

Unfair Treatment From Employers - Eeoc Home Page, http://www.eeoc.gov/employers/ (accessed November 14, 2017).

Want Your Employees To Trust You? Show You Trust Them, https://hbr.org/2017/07/want-your-employees-to-trust-you-show-you-trust-them (accessed November 11, 2017).

What Is A Peo? | Learn What To Expect From A Peo, https://www.insperity.com/blog/what-is-a-peo/ (accessed November 21, 2017).

Ibid.

What Is The Legal Working Age In Mount Pleasant, South .., https://answers.yahoo.com/question/index?qid=20070825070652AAxfzQr (accessed November 6, 2017).

Workers' Compensation - Wikipedia, https://en.wikipedia.org/wiki/Workers%E2%80%99_compensation (accessed November 14, 2017).

Workplace Posters - United States Department Of Labor, https://www.dol.gov/general/topics/posters (accessed November 15, 2017).

Why Does My Business Need An Employee Handbook, https://www.thebalance.com/why-does-my-company-need-an-employee-handbook-398090 (accessed November 15, 2017).

Ibid.

Your End-of-the Year Checklist — Getpayroll/simon, http://www.getpayroll.com/getpayrollblog/bp161220 (accessed November 17, 2017).

Ibid

Biographies

Charles Read
President/CEO of GetPayroll and the Simon™ Payroll App

MBA, CPA, USTCP, USMC, IRSAC

28-year Business Owner, IRS Watch Dog and Small Business Advocate

Charles Read is an accomplished senior executive and entrepreneur with more than 50 years of financial leadership experience in a broad range of industries, as well as a licensed Certified Public Accountant (CPA). His extensive background stretches across accounting, tax, manufacturing, construction, information technology, marketing, transportation, logistics, human resources, wholesale distribution, insurance, credit, and more. In addition, he is one of 86 people in the last 16 years to pass the US Tax Court Non-Attorney Practitioners Examination, which enables him to represent clients in the US Tax Court without being an attorney. Most recently, he was appointed by the IRS for their advisory council, Small Business Self-Employed/Wage & Investment.

Charles is not the typical CPA. He leverages his education, experience, and hard-earned wisdom to connect with individuals at every level within an organization. He creates impactful change as an advisor and solutions architect to resolve business-related challenges brought on by disruptive market forces and inefficient organizational planning. With a wealth of expertise as a CEO, CFO, COO, teacher, and consultant working in domestic and international markets, Charles is able to intuitively understand what a business needs to succeed and assist with laying out a strategic roadmap to accomplish that vision.

Devon Kirk
Director of Sales, Marketing, and Public Relations at GetPayroll Salon and Spa Marketing Expert, 30-year Licensed Esthetician, 7-year Day Spa Owner

Devon Kirk brings seven years experience as a business owner and 21 years experience in all aspects of B2B and B2C marketing. She has a degree in Information Technology in Business, and certifications in professional meeting planning, digital marketing, SEO, Google analytics, web, and graphic design. She was a national trainer for a cosmetic company for three years. She is currently completing her Masters in Science degree for Digital Marketing.

Devon has been a licensed esthetician for over 30 years and has been licensed in Pennsylvania, Delaware, Georgia, and Texas. She carries over 14 advanced industry certifications.